Best wishes.
Play BIG!

 12/2/11

Additional Praise for *Leadersh*t*:

"By combining his in-depth consulting experience with his personal journey, Mobley has written a stunningly original and riveting book about that most contentious and important topic, leadership."
— Warren Bennis
   Distinguished Professor of Management, University of
   Southern California and author of the recently published,
   Still Surprised: A Memoir of a Life in Leadership

"Foster Mobley has been a clear and compelling voice in the development of leaders for decades and has helped to shape the leadership cultures of many large organizations. Most important, Foster continues to learn and expand and offer the world his best thinking as is evidenced in this current book. If you are a leader you will find great guidance, reassurance and coaching in these pages."
— Dede Henley, Consultant and Author,
   The Secret of Sovereignty

"Whether your circle of influence is as broad as a Fortune 500 company or as local as a family, this book cuts through the cr*p and gets to the heart of leadership. Foster got this right!"
— Dr. Tracy Maylett, CEO, DecisionWise

"I've known Foster for years, and worried that his intense interest in leadership was misplaced. I was wrong. In these pages, Foster demonstrates that leadership is a behavior—not a position. It is a capacity that can be built in ourselves, our organizations, and our world, and with that capacity the possibility for great change."
> —Christopher G. Worley, Ph.D.,
> Senior Research Scientist, University of Southern California and Professor of Management, Pepperdine University

"Foster's wisdom has been instrumental in the development of leaders and teams across many organizations, including ours. He is both visionary and pragmatic—challenging us to examine our core beliefs and behaviors, and helping us lead more authentically and powerfully, enabling breakthrough results."
> —Andrew P. Hayek, Chief Executive Officer
> Surgical Care Affiliates

"Foster engages the mind as well as the heart of what it means to be a leader. He helps leaders navigate through challenging times, emerging more capable of influencing others to greatness."
> —Maritza G. Montiel,
> Deputy Chief Executive Officer, Deloitte

LEADERSH*T:

Rethinking the True Path to Great Leading

Leadersh*t

RETHINKING THE TRUE PATH TO GREAT LEADING

FOSTER W. MOBLEY, Ed.D.

Madison House Media
Los Angeles

Published by
Madison House Media
Los Angeles

www.madisonhousemedia.com

Cover design by Dunn+Associates, Inc., www.dunn-design.com
Interior design by Dorie McClelland, www.springbookdesign.com

ISBN: 978-0-9835299-0-3

To Cathy—my love and true companion.
To Erin, Lane and Maddi—my inspiration, my heart and my guides.

CONTENTS

Foreword ix

Introduction 3

ONE

The Tale of the Stream 17

TWO

The Tale of the Skipping Stones 47

THREE

The Tale of the Empty House 75

FOUR

The Tale of the Storm 109

FIVE

The Tale of the Old Bull 135

SIX

The Tale of the Trail 165

SEVEN

The Tale of the Spring 191

Acknowledgments 223

FOREWORD

I first became aware of Foster Mobley in 2008 through Sue Enquist, the former UCLA head softball coach. Sue told me that he had a refreshing way of saying simple things that rang true regardless of what sport you were in. I had been coaching for 20 years and had been very successful. During my tenure, we had won five NCAA championships, but we hadn't won a national championship in a while and I felt like I was saying the same things over and over. I didn't feel there was anything in particular I needed to fix, but I knew that I needed a fresh way of conveying what I believe are universal truths.

I am deeply blessed that the late, great John Wooden, the legendary UCLA basketball coach, was a friend and mentor to me. As anyone who spent time with Coach Wooden did, I learned a great many important truths from him. One of his keystones was what we often call the Golden Rule, though you can call it karma if you like. By any name, it's been around since the dawn of man. But the greatest gift I got from Coach Wooden was his definition of success. When I got this job, I was a gymnastics coach who had never done gymnastics—and yet I tried to be like every other successful gymnastics coach. Coach Wooden set me straight when he told me, "Success is the peace of mind that comes from knowing that you have done the best that *you* are capable of doing." Meaning, be yourself. Find your unique genius. Don't try to emulate others.

Working with Foster gave me practical ways to bring this wisdom to life. He didn't try to reinvent the wheel or to "fix" me with some system that he'd created but rather took universal truths and helped me turn them into something that my student athletes and I could relate to. He asked a lot of questions. He got me to ponder and verbalize things that I had never put words to. He posed tough questions about my coaching philosophy. I found myself struggling to describe my personal philosophy and morals. Foster also had me ask people who knew me well to describe what I do best—and also where I get into trouble and get in my own way. That was revealing, to say the least!

During this process, I discovered the power of Foster's central concept: clearing the stream. It's an idea that's very easy to convey, which is the hallmark of a universal truth. You don't need to ponder it a great deal to get its real meaning. I didn't have a lot of boulders in my stream from a coaching perspective, but the process allowed me to clear away the debris that was keeping me from having absolute clarity with my student athletes and coaching staff. He told me, "If you're not precise and clear about your intentions, then people will make them up." Having a picture of the stream in my mind, and clearing out the debris and trash, helped me become more of the leader that I could be.

Working with Foster as my coach has helped me shape my daily thought process as a person and a coach to others. He has helped me be less congested and clearer with my intentions and with the things I do on a daily basis. I'm a better leader by example because I am living my daily life by the same example. It all comes down to simplifying my thought process. That doesn't mean it's been easy or that I'm dumbing down my philosophy. Instead, I've cleared away what's unnecessary, allowing my stream to flow freely and powerfully. For example, in the past I felt that I had to be smarter than other coaches. I pressured myself to be on the cutting edge with technology and communications. I made things very complicated. I told myself that the smarter I was, the better a coach I could be. It was complexity for complexity's sake.

That was a way of dealing with insecurity. I hadn't won a championship in five years, but by inoculating myself against more potential failure, I was actually setting myself up to fail. By working with me to clear my stream, Foster helped me see that I already had some pretty sound philosophies that had been proven for thousands of years: work hard, be your best, focus on the moment, prepare. All I needed to do to make those philosophies work for my student athletes was to live them clearly and pristinely myself—not clutter them up, not make them complicated. If I wanted it to be a great day, I had to wake up and make it a great day.

In this book, you're going to get to know Foster, and you're going to discover someone who has taken decades to make something incredibly profound appear simple, gentle, and organic. In the time that I've known him, he's never pretended to have this wealth of secret knowledge that was never tapped before. He just has different ways of seeing things, accessing deep wisdom, and then communicating with language that makes sense to people and empowers them to take action.

Be prepared to be challenged and be honestly insightful about yourself. If you're not willing to be truly introspective, then don't bother reading further; you'll just waste your time. But if you are excited about looking at what you do well and learning to do it better, then he is a wonderful, transformative guide. He's not about soft-pedaling your strengths or weaknesses; he's about helping you find them and own them in a way that is empowering, not condescending. You won't feel stupid or foolish.

That's one of the most extraordinary things about Foster: he's virtually without ego. He's not concerned about being the all-knowing solution. He doesn't swoop in with a system of tools and methods that you have to adopt to "fix" yourself. From his perspective, you're not broken. There's nothing necessary for leading that you don't already have in you. All he does is reveal the genius within you and help you be completely yourself rather than try to emulate anyone else. It's a fun, enlightening and enriching process . . . if you're ready for it.

What I love most about Foster's process is that there is no magic equation. No "X habits for successful leading." No ten-step program. No potion that will immediately make me 100 percent successful in everything I do. If you've read enough leadership books and attended enough seminars, you know that such things don't exist. They are nothing more than sales tools. With Foster, you do the work. You're rediscovering yourself with each question and each answer. He's there to guide you, help you find the things that are getting in the way of your stream, be your authentic self, be fully present in the moment, and become the leader you have always been capable of being.

I feel that my well of leadership is deep, and I look forward to working with Foster throughout my career. I'm not finished by a long shot. There is much fine-tuning to come, and I see this as a career-long relationship. We have won one NCAA championship together, and I see many more rings in our future!

Foster has been a blessing to me as I continue on this glorious journey. If you can shed the old models and ideas about leading and listen to his quiet, clear voice, I am confident that he will be the same to you on your journey.

Valorie Kondos Field
Head Coach, UCLA Gymnastics
August 2011

LEADERSH*T:

Rethinking the True Path to Great Leading

INTRODUCTION

It is unwise to be too sure of one's own wisdom. It is healthy to be
reminded that the strongest might weaken and the wisest might err.
—Gandhi

He was a small, slender man, perhaps five foot four or an inch taller.
He could have been fifty years old. Or forty. Or sixty-five; it was
impossible to tell. He had brown, sun-weathered skin that gave lie
to his residence in the sun-starved Pacific Northwest. His hair was
close-cropped, so I couldn't discern its color. When I first saw him,
he was wearing a leather Harley-Davidson cap and smoking one of
those "all natural" cigarettes like Native Spirit. It was like meeting
a character taken, immediate and breathing, from a scene in *Easy
Rider*. But he was real, and he was part of the inspiration for this
book. His name was Sawyer.

I met Sawyer upon gathering with dear family friends after the
sudden and tragic loss of their daughter, Carly. As a huge outpour-
ing of friends and relations converged on the bereaved at their
home in suburban Seattle, several men gathered to grieve, meditate,
and heal through a uniquely male ritual: the Native American sweat
lodge. If you have never experienced a sweat lodge, it's quite primal.
The gathered men work together to build a small, temporary lodge
in which they congregate, strip down to their shorts or skivvies, and
sit in communion for hours. In the center of the floor are "grandfather stones"; a sacred fire is kindled under them outside the lodge,

and after they are white-hot, they are carefully delivered into the lodge where a water pourer douses them with water periodically to create a scalding steam that makes the lodge positively oppressive. The men sit in this dark, quiet, sweltering haven and share stories, hear wisdom from elders, and purify themselves.

Sawyer, an elder in the ManKind Project community and trained in Native American language and ritual, directed our crew in building our sweat lodge with simple, clipped instructions: "Over there," and "Do it this way." When the lodge was complete, we entered and began the process of stripping away our defenses and our attachments—of becoming fully present to our own fears and grief so that we could help my friend both bear and shed his sorrow. Sawyer now became our water pourer and master of ceremonies. He led the rituals and songs that sounded as if they came from the earth itself. His tone and mood were serious and thoughtful, but not somber. He was as grounded as an oak and completely comfortable with the spiritual.

With his leadership, we engaged in songs and blessings and released our cries to the universe. We welcomed the spirits to our sacred space, and when we shared stories between songs, Sawyer maintained the narrative thread. His perspective on life and death was extraordinary: "We are all connected to each other, and all men are my fathers and grandfathers," he would say. He would speak of animals as equals, referring to them as "the four-legged ones" or "the ones that fly." He blew apart our closely held myths about death, spirit, and our ownership of our bodies.

"This young woman who has passed, we don't use her name, out of respect," he said at one point. "Some said that she lived a short life. But in my tradition, she lived a life. Who can know that twenty years is too short? That is our judgment of what a full life can be. She lived as full a life in those years as any of us have lived in our bodies. Spirit does not have an end." It was like sitting in the presence of an ancient sage, a real-world Gandalf without the long beard.

4

After some time, helpers brought in more grandfather stones until there were about forty stones in all. We were positively broiling in the lodge. I looked at Sawyer, lit by the glowing stones, and thought, "This guy could be sixty years old; he's going to drop dead in this heat." Instead, he looked utterly content, totally present, and perfectly centered. In ninety minutes, he took a grieving father and stepfather, along with brothers, stepbrothers, and friends, and transformed our states of mind through simple statements, elemental rituals, and his profound presence.

When we gratefully emerged dripping wet from the lodge into the cool air, Sawyer said little. He toweled off, made arrangements to pick up the lodge on another day, dropped his Harley cap on his head, lit one of his smokes, climbed into his truck, and took off. I was completely taken by this character. It would have been incredibly easy to prejudge him as some blue-collar laborer with his cigarettes and his truck, and I didn't doubt that many people had dismissed him as exactly that without a second thought.

Their loss. As soon as he opened his mouth, it was clear that this was a man who was and is completely present in head, hands, heart, and spirit. He was content with how he walked on this earth and with being precisely who he was. He didn't just utter wisdom; he was wisdom. I spent two hours with the man and I will never forget him.

277,000 and Counting

Sawyer was a leader in the truest of senses—in who and what he was, not just in what he did. By example, he showed the rest of us how we could choose to find our own meaning in the tragedy we were mourning. Sawyer came to vivid life in my mind when I set out to write *Leadersh*t: Rethinking the True Path to Great Leading.*

As I was thinking about the kind of book I wanted to write, it was clear what I didn't want to write: a clone of the approximately

277,000 other books on leading and leadership that already clog bookstore shelves like plaque in coronary arteries. There are some important foundational concepts in some of those books, and yet most are guilty of a multitude of sins: promoting the latest business-school trends, propagating ridiculous myths, or rehashing warmed-over advice about motivation and vision-setting.

I also didn't want my book to be another preachy how-to manual pushing a trademarked one-size-fits-all solution. I wanted to cut through the deafening clatter and impossible clutter and bring people something true and transformative. I knew I wasn't going to do that by writing another book filled with steps and processes. No two organizations, or people, are alike. Could I develop a proprietary multi-step program or method that would apply to everybody from CEOs to mid-level managers from any organization and magically turn them into effective leaders? Of course not. It would be arrogance to assume that I could.

I also knew that I wasn't just writing for occupants of the C-suite. First-level supervisors are leaders, too. So are the moms who run Girl Scout troops. So are sports coaches and teachers. Parents might be the most important and least rewarded leaders of all time. I wanted to speak to them as well, because their wisdom often comes closer to the heart of what I teach than all the material from a hundred corporate seminars and how-to methodologies.

Then I remembered Sawyer, who so embodied the approach I use in my work with leaders. I call it Wisdom Leading™. Just as he had shared timeless truths about the self and spirit with the men in the sweat lodge, I wanted to share timeless truths about what it takes to perform at your best and encourage greatness from others—truths that apply whether you're a CEO or a choral director and whether you're running a billion-dollar, private-equity-owned healthcare firm or coaching a junior-college baseball team. I imagined what it would be like to spend a few days with someone like Sawyer, just listening and learning. And just like that, I had it.

So it is that on the coming pages you will encounter a Foster Mobley you may not have seen or heard before. By envisioning myself on a classic road trip with a wise man very much like Sawyer, I believe I have tapped into a voice unlike anything in those other 277,000 books: calm, reasoned, and wise, with a focus on *leading*—the fundamental connection of self and others—not *leadership*, an overworked and confusing jumble of issues surrounding position, power, and heroic financial or technical exploits. I'm less interested in stories about people who, due to their financial acumen or technological breakthroughs, grace the covers of *Fortune* and *Businessweek*. Instead, I have attempted to craft a storytelling framework that will encourage you to explore the emotional, psychological and spiritual borderlands of what it means to be a *leader* of people. You be the judge of whether or not I've done my job.

Leading Versus Leadersh*t

Before we get into it, let's talk about leading as opposed to leadersh*t. To me, *leading* means *building capacity in yourself and others to create breakthrough results*. However, in thirty-plus years as a consultant, speaker, and executive coach, I have found myself increasingly frustrated with the misguided nature of much of what goes by the innocuous name "leadership"—what I call leadersh*t.

Whatever you call it, it's not working very well. A global survey of 836 senior managers in Australia, Denmark, Germany, France, Great Britain, Italy, India, Sweden, Switzerland, and the United States, conducted in June 2010 by executive search firm Egon Zehnder International, showed that nearly 70 percent of executives believe corporate leaders lack basic business competencies and innovation skills as well as the ability to drive change and customer focus. A December 2008 global survey of 828 senior executives by Booz & Company found that 40 percent doubted their corporate leaders had a plan to weather the recession, while 46 percent said that even if such a plan were in place, they doubted their leaders had the ability to execute it. Finally, according to a 2007 Towers Perrin survey of nearly 9,000 workers around the world, only 21 percent felt fully engaged at work, while 40 percent felt disengaged or disenchanted.

Despite this, for decades the greatest theoreticians in leadership and organization development have preached a gospel based on the same basic ideas: if executives and companies master a set of new processes, methods, or tools, they will be able to motivate, organize, and inspire their people and turn dysfunctional businesses into superpowers. I divide these experts into four categories:

1. *The Econo-Stars*—These include Jack Welch of GE, Larry Bossidy of Allied Signal, and Andy Grove of Intel. They'll tell you how they did it and how you should emulate what they did to confront turbulent times.

2. *The Consul-Stars*—These include Ram Charan, Jim Kouzes and Barry Posner, and Stephen Covey and Ken Blanchard. Each of these thinkers provides a collection of "answers" that focuses on the success paths of others, told through compelling anecdotes, and suggests a partial, one-size-fits-all solution.

3. *Academic/Literary Stars*—Warren Bennis, John Kotter, Rosabeth Moss Kanter, John W. Gardner and many others contribute extensive research and historical perspectives, laying the foundation for much of what we know today as the accepted frameworks for business and societal leadership.

4. *Mythologists*—Such luminaries as Spencer Johnson, MD (of *Who Moved My Cheese?* fame) and Patrick Lencioni (*Five Temptations of a CEO*) use parables to break down one small aspect of a very complex issue and offer a comforting prescription.

I stand on the shoulders of these giants. Throughout my career, I have walked from the thoughts and insights of one to the next like a boy crossing a pond on stepping-stones. Exposure to each leadership worldview and methodology has sparked questions and provoked new thinking. I'm in their debt.

And here's the thing: Every one of them is wrong about what makes a great leader.

Leadersh*t is my catchall term for the myths, lazy thinking, misconceptions, and product marketing that distract individuals from doing the cognitive heavy lifting that produces powerful performance and lasting, positive change. Confusion is rampant in this field because there are few standards. What makes a great leader? How do you build one? Are the best leaders born? Made? Do you become one by mastering a set of skills, competencies, processes, and systems, as the myriad books and trainers suggest? Because there is no consensus on what leadership means or what works, flavor-of-the-month initiatives and generic solutions rule the day. The author with the trendiest book or the company with the most convincing sales pitch wins . . . *whether or not their ideas have any positive impact on the individual's or the company's performance.*

Charisma, skills, competencies, and processes may matter, but they take a back seat to mindful presence, calm, wisdom, and self-awareness. Effective leading begins with personal transformation—with knowing and nurturing your senses of purpose and meaning and the source of your vitality. For me it's this simple: the journey to powerful leading always goes through the self. Despite its contrarian title, *Leadersh*t: Rethinking the True Path to Great Leading* represents my life's commitment to the discovery and practice of powerful leading and performance. It presents an empowering, effective alternative to the junk methods that make people and organizations *feel* as though they are taking bold steps toward the future when in reality they are wasting time and money trying to fix what isn't broken. You already have everything you need to be a more effective leader.

A Gift of Wisdom

I'm a teacher and a storyteller at heart, so I'm going to share my truths about how to discover and release those effective-leading qualities primarily through story. A storyteller's job is to take themes that may be deep and complex and simplify them into a narrative that is resonant and unforgettable. That's what I've tried to do here—take wisdom that I've discovered and developed over thirty years of work with more than 25,000 clients and reduce it to something quiet, simple, and clear as a bell.

As I've said, I call my approach Wisdom Leading. It's the opposite of leadersh*t, the method- and process-oriented snake oil that so many books and development programs pitch. That approach insists that the only way to become a great leader is to graft various skill sets, processes, and systems onto yourself, often at great expense.

In contrast, Wisdom Leading says that you *already possess* everything you need to be an effective leader. If you can wrap your brain around that, try this: the inescapable secret is that the shortest distance between where you are and breakthrough results is learning to get out of your own way—to remove the obstacles that prevent you from accessing the wisdom and greatness that you already possess. It's about allowing your *essence*—who you are when you are at your best—to come through for the people you lead.

Through the course of *Leadersh*t: Rethinking the True Path to Great Leading*, I'm going to share and explore with you seven metaphors that represent simple ways to access fundamental states of mind and *being* (read this as "how you show up") critical to great leading. This is ancient knowledge that's been around for as long as civilization. It's not new or trendy. What is new, however, are these simple ways to think about and access your own wisdom and experience without reading the original Sanskrit version of the *Bhagavad Gita*. Many people are quick to relegate wisdom to esoteric religious philosophy or see it as distant and confounding, but it really is part of our common intellectual heritage. These seven "access points" are ready for you to explore and put to good use:

1. The Stream
2. The Skipping Stone
3. The Empty House
4. The Storm
5. The Old Bull
6. The Trail
7. The Spring

After committing my life to exploring every nook and cranny of the leadership landscape, I'm finally able to offer a great gift: the distillation of these 25,000-plus learning moments with leaders around the globe, gathered over three decades of fieldwork and hands-on experience. As you know, it takes hard work to make the complex appear simple and approachable, and that's what I've tried to do here. My mission is to give anyone who is in a position to lead others—which is to say almost everyone—a toolkit to "stop the insanity" of leadersh*t and find his or her own unique brilliance as a leader.

I've got one more gift to offer: I am one of the few leadership coaches who has worked both with top business leaders and championship sports teams. So I share not only examples from the world of business but strategies and ideas from the world of high-pressure, elite-level collegiate athletics. It's a world where the pressure is on, there's nowhere to hide, and outcomes mean everything, and it's been some of the most personally rewarding work of my entire career. I'll share with you the stories and the results, which are not only inspiring but translate beautifully from the gymnasium to the boardroom and back again!

Myths and Misconceptions

Before you can appreciate why Wisdom Leading works so well, it's important that you understand clearly what *doesn't* work. So I'd like to beg your indulgence and spend a few minutes on some of the misconceptions that have become part of the accepted body of leadership knowledge. Let's bust a few myths:

• *Leading is reserved for the Chosen.* We cling to this idea that title, position, birthright, or degree somehow confers the ability to lead. Under this misguided notion, only certain individuals possess the traits of a leader, while the rest of us are left to struggle in the wake of genius like an NBA bench player substituting for Michael Jordan.

In truth, the contents of your gene pool and where you went to school are the wrong considerations. Your birthright may get you into the Skull and Bones society at Yale, but it bypasses the central focus of this book about how well you lead others. Anyone who leads another is a leader. The right (and only) question is how good you are at it. My experience tells me that most of us have the potential to be exceptional leaders given the right environment, goals, and challenges, and that we all bear the seeds of genius and need only the proper conditions to make them grow.

• *Leading is external.* If you aren't leading effectively, it's the fault of the talent around you, the organization, the economy, or some other cause outside of you, right? This is the ultimate self-delusion, because it encourages people and companies to look everywhere for the "fix" except where the problem truly lies: with the person doing the leading. When it comes to leading others, there is no "out there."

Success or failure as a leader is always about you. Everything begins with the character, focus, commitment, and example of the individual who claims the leader's mantle. Leadership is in the eyes of the led; those you lead will show *with their performance* whether you're getting the job done or not.

• *Leaders separate their work and personal lives.* Who decided that we could or should be different people at home and at work? Many organizations' cultures fear that acknowledging the importance of our passions, health, or families will cause us to lose our edge as tough-minded leaders. I regularly see the harmful effects of work environments that ignore the deeper human needs of their people: stress-related health problems, high turnover and absenteeism, low morale, and "presenteeism," where people are on the job but not present in mind and not performing at anything near their peak.

Frankly, this one has taken me a long time to understand (especially as a recovering MBA), but my experience and work strongly refute this myth. My dear friend and mentor Dede Henley says, "What you do anywhere is what you do everywhere." When the leaders I work with access their deep wisdom, they make profound changes that lead to better on-the-job performance and greater personal fulfillment for themselves and others. Their approaches to both work *and* life change, and that's what produces the phenomenal results I see. You cannot shut yourself off as a human being and put yourself into some sort of work-only gear and expect to function optimally. There is no such thing as a work-only gear.

There is just you.

• *There is a "leader personality."* There's an assumption that people with natural charisma, speaking ability, or abundant stores of energy make the best leaders. Wrong. The most important communication occurs not at a podium during a shareholders meeting but at the water cooler (or in the locker room after a painful loss), where the leader's integrity, authenticity, commitment, and presence are on display. The most important charisma (defined as attractiveness or charm) is whatever connects leaders and followers, no matter the style. We need to wrestle this to the ground right here: there is no best "leader type"—or "parent type" or "coaching style," either.

- *Leading is about competencies.* If you have endured multi-day seminars and leadership boot camps and flipped through binders full of information about vision, goals, or delegation until your fingers bled, blame this myth. It tells us that organizing, setting goals, and holding better meetings make up the DNA of leading.

Those might be necessary managerial tools, but they come into play downstream from the personal transformation and connection that must happen before breakthrough leading can occur. You can only make use of them after you have "become the change you wish to see" in your organization. Until then, building on competencies is like laying bricks to build a house without pouring a foundation. Here's the simple truth: you must first start with you. When you can lead yourself successfully, then you've earned the right to lead others, regardless of what your job description says.

How to Read this Book

This book is about reality, not theory or myth, and can serve a reader on multiple levels. Each chapter will begin with a narrative describing the fictional journey I am undertaking along with the Wise Man, my Sawyer surrogate and the bearer of knowledge about life and leading that surpasses my own. During each stage of our travels through the backcountry, we encounter an obstacle or situation that physically represents one of my seven access points to powerful, wise leading. Along the way, we discuss the meaning of these experiences and provide some nifty visual and educational metaphors. Anyone (i.e., mom, dad, boss, coach) can read the first third of each chapter—the on-the-road adventure—and walk away with a good sense of the key lessons.

From these symbolic adventures, each chapter transitions into a one-to-one discussion of the relevant aspect of Wisdom Leading. This is the more conventional and completely practical part of the book: storytelling, citing examples from some of my clients, and expanding on critical concepts related to meaning, mindfulness, change, and distraction. My approach and message are a bit unconventional, but I am also well aware that while you're bringing out the greatness of your followers, at the end of the day the trains have to run on time. I've run a company for thirty years. I've had to make payroll every two weeks. I get it. Everything here can be put into action immediately.

Each chapter concludes with a collection of questions I call Access Points. These aren't review questions but something different: powerful and disquieting questions I've been asked by a coach or mentor or have asked coaching clients in guiding their journeys. I encourage you to reflect on them, be clear with yourself about your answers, and/or compose your own questions in the same vein and answer them as completely and honestly as you can. It isn't easy to wean yourself off the "following the checklist" paradigms of leadersh*t. Access Points will help you begin detoxing by placing the ownership for your own journey back where it belongs.

The Takeaway

The poet e.e. cummings wrote, "All ignorance toboggans into know and trudges up to ignorance again . . ." Learning how to be a leader is not a college course with a distinct beginning and end. If you approach it from within—the only true vantage point for leading— your evolution into a breakthrough leader will occur in the same way that you develop as a human being: in cycles of insight, humility, and rediscovery. Challenges often present themselves when you're least ready for them; this book is a primer on how to be more ready and aware.

Sir Ernest Shackleton, who led the ill-fated 1914 Antarctic exploration that became one of the most incredible survival stories in human history, said, "Difficulties are just things to overcome, after all." Brave words. But in reality, no one had any idea that Shackleton would be the kind of leader who could lead his men over 800 miles of open sea from certain death on their icebound ship *Endurance* to a barren island and eventual survival *without losing a single crew member.* He was a failure in his business ventures on land and not a "great leader" by any of the usual metrics such as wartime medals or advanced degrees. Yet something within him enabled him to keep morale up in impossible circumstances, motivate his men to take the most extraordinary risks, and keep everyone alive.

What I'm teaching is not new. It is much older than today's life, with its fragmentary attention spans and nanosecond time scale. Mindfulness, presence, accountability—these are things we have always known; we've just forgotten them. But that knowledge doesn't die. It goes dormant like plant bulbs in the frozen ground, waiting for sunshine until they bloom again. You are not broken; you don't need a transfusion of some leadership system. You have always had what it takes.

Great leading is about showing up powerfully. It's about commitment and engagement. It's about head and hands but also about heart, purpose, and spirit. It is about knowing yourself and being fully in the moment so that when the moments of critical performance come, you can evoke the very best in yourself and in others. The rest is just leadersh*t.

Now sit back while I tell you a story . . .

ONE

The Tale of the Stream

Character develops itself in the stream of life.
—Johann Wolfgang von Goethe

here's something sensual about the natural bank and curve of a trail as it crests a rise and dips into a wooded glen filled with ferns and the trickle of water. I think such a scene appeals to something primal that lies deeply buried in the human psyche—to our native longing for a secret quiet place, or perhaps our brains' hunger for the scents of minerals, tree resin, and chill fog. The trail that crackled softly beneath my boots was filled with such atmosphere.

But mostly, it was a lot of damned hard work.

I was deep in the backcountry of—well, let's not limit your imagination by tethering it to a specific part of the continent. It's enough to know that I was far enough from civilization to feel the truth of my own smallness, surrounded by a silence so profound that my inner voice, a bit atrophied after years of speaking, listening, analyzing, and consulting, began to crack its knuckles, limber up its synapses and amaze me with spontaneous flights of fancy on life, the universe, and whether Pete Rose should be in the Baseball Hall of Fame. Blown leaves thundered about me as I descended into —"Mind you don't fall behind, son."

Ah, yes. My personal reality check had opened up a fifty-yard gap on me, moving at a pace that was all the more amazing given the fact that he had at least fifteen years on me and was carrying twice the weight in his pack. I stepped up my pace.

At this point, some backstory is in order. I had been minding my own business after spending several days minding other people's business, which is what I have done for three decades. I had been consulting with a company about developing a culture of engagement and performance, and after four days of presentations to people who seemed to think I had something meaningful to say, I was exhausted. I had come to a lakeside town in the foothills to spend a quiet night and take an easy hike the next day to clear my head before heading for the airport and home. But as I sat in a cozy local pub that evening, I'd noticed this gentleman drinking alone and invited him to join me.

What ensued was one of the most astonishing conversations I've ever enjoyed. He seemed to have been everywhere, done everything, and known virtually everyone, from the Rat Pack to Woody Guthrie to John Updike. Lean, spare, and ageless, with a neatly cropped beard and short silver hair, he had the classic Nordic profile of someone whose ancestors had reached these shores with Eric the Red. I think he was about seventy, but he could have been the age of my father or my grandfather; it was impossible to tell. Once I told him what I did for a living, our intended couple of local ales quickly became a food-and-drink-fueled, up-till-closing-time dialogue about leaders and vision and human behavior.

"Leadership?" he said over what must have been his tenth drink of the evening, though he showed no signs of intoxication. The fire crackled into the space between his sentences.

"More like leadershit, son," he said. "Most people who claim to be leaders don't have the slightest idea what that means. They think it's about making speeches and setting goals." He shook his head and I noticed a gold hoop glinting in his left earlobe. "It ain't. Real leading is about who you are."

Since I built my work around precisely the same philosophy, I started to ask him what had led him to this conclusion; in my experience, it was rare for anyone to think in this way. The words had barely started tumbling out of my mouth when he held up a hand and gently stopped me. His manner was calm and self-contained; he saw no need to raise his voice. Instead, he held my attention completely with a direct, piercing gaze from under the brim of his weather-beaten leather Harley-Davidson cap.

19

"It's not something I can tell you," he said. His eyes gleamed as a small smile formed on his lips. "But I can show you." He asked me to join him on an odyssey that was, for him, strictly minor-league: a trek through early autumn hills between small towns about 120 miles apart. In return for my company, he said, he would share with me all he had learned about the act of leading. I had little on my agenda for when I got back to the office, and this was simply too tempting to resist. As the innkeeper hustled us out into the early morning cold (we had talked until 1 a.m., though I had no idea how), I shook his hand and said, "I'm in." He told me to pack sturdy boots, warm clothes, and enough food for a seven-day hike and promised to meet me at my hotel the next morning after breakfast. Then he climbed into an ancient Ford truck and rattled away.

The Journey Begins

The next morning, I emerged from my hotel rested but apprehensive. I had the requisite pack, clothes, and boots, but I felt uneasy. What had I signed on for? Was I heading into the woods with a crazy mountain man who would try to ax-murder me when my back was turned? Visions of The Blair Witch Project danced through my head.

Then I walked out into the bright sunshine and saw the Wise Man leaning against one of the posts that held up the long wooden porch. He was shaking out his boot. "Even a journey of a thousand miles begins with . . . a rock in the shoe," he said. "Ow." Finally, a small pebble rolled out and he slipped his boot back on.

"Of such inauspicious beginnings are epics begun," I quipped as I hoisted my backpack higher on my shoulders. His pack was prehistoric canvas and at least twice the size of mine. He hefted it with ease, shot me a raised eyebrow and then grabbed his walking stick and led the way. I followed down the hill through thigh-high rushes of golden-dried grasses to the trail that we would take for many days. Our journey was underway.

The Wise Man set the pace. Why do I call him that? Because he would never tell me his name, and I have to call him something. But it suited him. He radiated a sense of ancient knowledge, of total acceptance of everything around him, as though he had seen it at all before. He just took it all in and was completely in the present. Rain, wind, bear tracks, a sore knee—they were all parts of a larger whole, each glorious in its own way.

The hard work came in trying to keep up. My companion was lithe and quick on his feet, apparently accustomed to navigating the bumps and rolls that come even on a well-kept trail like the one we hiked. He moved effortlessly; I moved less so, and I lost ground steadily until he had to call back to me as I moved down into the saddle of a deep dell and then trudged out the other side. The first day of a hike always makes your body feel as if it's been put together by nearsighted giants. I huffed and puffed my way up to where he stood, a thin smile on his face.

"I'll slow down a bit so we can make conversation," he said, then winked and set off again between twin rows of young birches that looked like soldiers standing at attention. I only hoped the conversation would be worth the mild humiliation. I stayed off his right shoulder, about ten yards back.

Five quiet minutes ticked by. "Why are you following me?" he said suddenly. Meaning and layers, meaning and layers, I reminded myself. Get past the surface.

"Because you know the way."

"Sure, but you didn't have to come with me. You had other plans. Why are you following me?"

Why does one follow a leader? What makes a follower? I got his meaning right away: I had chosen to change my plans because I was curious about what he knew. It was as he had said; I wasn't following because of anything he had done but because of some ineffable sense of who he was. Perhaps the defining characteristic of followers is the desire to learn and grow at the hands of someone who possesses a perspective on the world that they lack.

"I don't know yet," I finally answered.

He looked over his shoulder. "I like that, especially the 'yet' part. It's a smart man who knows enough to admit that he doesn't know."

The trail emerged from a thick stand of alder and ash trees. Before us wound a stream in a deep cut at least twelve feet across, a long red gash in the iron-rich soil. It descended from the hills where we had just walked and tumbled its way down a slow grade, presumably to merge with a larger watercourse somewhere beyond the woodlands. The Wise Man slowed for a moment to check his map and then strode briskly toward a timber bridge that spanned the creek.

But when we reached the middle of the bridge and looked down, the sight was puzzling. It was early fall and summer was not long past, but there had been rain in these parts not a week before; the ground was still spongy and mossy from it. Yet the stream was nearly dry. Dead fish littered its bed, soda cans glinted in the sun, and a fishing pole was stuck vertically into a muddy patch by the shore, presumably abandoned by a frustrated fisherman.

My companion was as puzzled as I was. "This stream ain't itself," he said, looking upstream from the center of the span. "It should be running clean and swift, at least three or four feet deep this time of year."

"Maybe someone diverted the water," I speculated.

He shook his head. "No farms anywhere near here. Nope, something's blocking the water flow." He turned to me with a gleam in his eye. "We're going to clear this stream."

The Descent

We were hiking overland, upstream, trail blazing in what had become an uncomfortably warm sun. The Wise Man, unperturbed as always, took a fallen alder branch and used it as a walking stick to pick out a clear and solid way up the stream's banks.

"Why are we doing this, again?" I asked, struggling to keep up.

He slowed until we were walking shoulder to shoulder. "Tell me, son, what's the relationship between the land around this stream and the stream itself?"

"Well, I suppose you could compare it to a body," I said. "The land is the body and the stream is the circulatory system bringing what the land needs to live." Sounded plausible, but I was really on my heels, just learning how the man thought.

To my satisfaction, he nodded. "That's right. Another way to say it would be that all the activity that takes place around the streambed is dependent on the flow of the water," he said. He led me around the carcass of a junked car buried so deep in decades-old weeds that it was nearly invisible. "Fish, turtles, amphibians, and birds depend on the stream for food and life itself. Somewhere down-stream, a small farm or cottage might depend on its water to recharge a well. Kids depend on it so they can go fishing, birders and hikers like us do so we have water to drink and pretty sights to see, and of course all these plants rely on that flow to survive."

The watercourse turned sharply to the north and the ground became steeper. The rushes and grasses were knee high and yellow after the summer's heat. I looked into the stream and the water was barely flowing. Other objects lay exposed to the sun: a tortoiseshell comb, a baseball, a bicycle tire. We seemed to be drawing closer to the blockage, and I wanted to get at the core of what the Wise Man was talking about before physical labor stemmed his flow of thoughts.

"So, nothing can happen without that flow of water being free and open," I said. "Right." He pointed upstream about a mile—a long, hot, uphill mile. His eyes were apparently as keen as his mind, because I couldn't make out any detail at that distance. "That's where we need to go. That's where we'll find what's blocking this stream."

I suggested that rather than blaze our own trail through the rough landscape, we should actually walk in the streambed. It was, after all, virtually empty and nearly bone-dry. "Capital idea!" he shouted. "Right to the heart of the matter!" In three strides, he stepped into space and vanished from my sight. Panicked, I ran to the edge of the deep bed, certain I would see him sprawled at the bottom with a broken leg . . . but he was bounding down the steep bank like a mountain goat, digging his heels into the dry earth for traction until he stood at the bottom, smiling up at me.

"Try it! Lean back for balance and don't look down!" he called. "Don't think, just do!" I prayed that a 911 call on my cell phone would go through and stepped down the bank. I cleared my mind of my fear and trepidation and simply let gravity carry me down the firm soil. I wasn't graceful, but in ten seconds I was standing beside my companion, grinning as though I'd just done something momentous.

"Well done," he said. "How did you do that?"

How had I done it? It had been an intimidating descent, but when I stepped onto the bank, my mind had been clear of thoughts of broken ankles and shattering, ass-over-tea-kettle crashes. I'd refused to attach any meaning or implication to the stream bank and just done it without fear, really without thought.

He smiled as we walked. "Thoughts, worries, fears, guilt: it's all debris, son," he said. "This stream we're walking in makes all the things that happen downstream possible. It doesn't matter where the water comes from; as long as it flows, it becomes the reason for the life and activity downstream. Unless something blocks the water, that is."

Clearing the Stream

Something had done just that. At a sharp elbow bend in the watercourse, a sycamore tree had come unmoored from its roots, perhaps during a summer storm, and tumbled into the stream, leaving only its roots still resting on the bank. A barricade had collected around its crown of branches and leaves: twigs and rushes, mud and sand, a school desk, and a basketball backboard, of all things. But at the heart of this accidental dam was a boulder at least two feet wide, wedged like a cork in a bottle. Behind the mess, the water of the stream collected and pooled, spreading from bank to bank and barely trickling through the blockage to head downstream. Like a blocked artery, the blocked stream was harming the life that depended on it.

This was no two-man job, I decided. This was a job for a road crew with a backhoe and chainsaws. But as I stood pondering, the Wise Man was moving.

"See?" he said, pointing at the boulder. "That rock is the clog. It's keeping this stream from completely being what it's supposed to be. It's not meant to be a dry slash in the ground. This is an ecosystem and a playground. We move that rock, we start the water flowing again."

I was less than impressed. "We also get inundated by muddy water and pieces of floating junk, you know," I replied. Then it hit me: clearing that stream to allow the water to flow and the stream to return to its natural state and purpose was the same as someone removing fear, anxiety, or misplaced meaning from a situation so innate capacity and passion could come through! Both were about getting the crap out of the way.

"No, you're right," I said. "Let's do it." He didn't say a word, just winked at me and turned to the barrier of junk nearly ten feet across. He shoved his shoulder against the rock. No luck. "That thing must weigh two hundred pounds," I said.

He stopped and stroked his stubbly beard, glaring at the stone as though his gaze could shatter it. Then he picked up his makeshift walking stick. I did the same, taking up a long pole that must have been a discarded fencepost. Together, we wedged our sticks under opposite sides of the massive stone and, on a silent signal, began rocking it back and forth. Slowly, gradually, it began to tilt to one side, then the other, each tilt building up momentum that carried it farther on the opposite side. Finally, the lean grew great enough that the stone tipped beyond its balance and fell toward my legs. I jumped out of the way as it rolled several times—and then I was in the flow of muddy water that quickly filled the channel up to shin depth and, after a few moments, was running clear.

My companion and I leaned on our sticks, caught our breath, and looked at each other. Then we began to laugh for a reason I can't really describe. It just felt right.

"C'mon," he said after a minute and moved toward the furniture and other debris still blocking the watercourse. We heaved and hoed desks, tree limbs, and boxes to the side, freeing more room for the natural water flow to resume. When the stream had reclaimed much of its bed and risen to our thighs, I said, "I think it's time we left this to Mother Nature."

He nodded, and we slogged our way to the bank and climbed up to dry land. I removed my muddy boots and decanted enough water from them to fill a goldfish bowl, then looked back at the stream. It was a living thing again, moving slowly but steadily with silty but clean water. I had no idea if the stream had a name, but did it matter?

"We did a good thing," I said.

"Yep," he said, setting his boots on a rock to dry in the warm sun. "Now the things and people downstream will follow the stream's lead and become what they were supposed to be again." He glanced over at me. "That's how it works, you know."

I laughed to myself. "Lesson in leading, number one?"

"You said it; I didn't."

We sat back against the trunk of a tree to wait for our footwear to dry out. Later, we would cover our final miles before finding shelter for the night.

My Thoughts on The Tale of the Stream

In this section, I'm going to present thoughts and examples of what I consider to be a central and fundamental aspect of Wisdom Leading: clearing away obstacles to your power. In Buddhist theology, the stream is a metaphor for the natural flow of energy, passions, and talents in each of us, and as I'll describe, it is vital to any leader's effectiveness. And it's quite easy to allow that flow to become obstructed. When that occurs, breakthrough leading and results become impossible. In this chapter, I'll present my case for why this is so and share some methods for keeping your stream flowing clear and strong. As I would with a coaching client, I'll invite you to sit beside me, shoulder to shoulder, as we explore together the most powerful concepts I know for the transformation of leaders and their performance.

We are complex beings. We are as much creatures of the mind, heart, and spirit as of the body; all four demand care if we are to function optimally as leaders or followers. That is the core thesis of this book.

It's appropriate that I begin sharing my direct message with you by telling a story of my own journey. In 1966, forty-five years ago, I was eleven years old. Like today, 1966 was a time of turbulent change, marked by global instability and tension, war, social unrest, and political divisiveness. Bob Dylan, the poet laureate of the age, sang, "Your old road is rapidly agin'. Please get out of the new one if you can't lend your hand, for the times they are a-changin.'" As my friends and clients know, I decided to pursue a doctoral degree later in life, in the field in which I'd practiced for nearly twenty-five years by that time. In my very first week of study, I read an article written in 1966 by a man, now a friend, I consider to be a titan of leadership thinking: Warren Bennis. In that article, he wrote, "The true hope for man . . . lay in his ability to rationalize, to calculate, and to use his head, as well as his hands and heart." From 1966. Genius.

ISDOM LEADING CONCEPTS

- Your stream is the natural expression of your unique talents, energies, passions, and experiences

- Many things like habits, fears, and self-limiting beliefs block your stream

- A blocked stream impedes your ability to lead yourself and others effectively

- The starting point in Wisdom Leading is understanding that you are NOT broken and you have everything you need to lead brilliantly

- How you "show up" as a leader is often far more important than what you do or say

ISDOM LEADING GOALS

- Understanding what your stream is and how it becomes obstructed

- Knowing the impact of a blocked stream on your followers and organization

- Learning how to identify your boulders and unblock your stream

- Learning how to show up powerfully for your people

I tell this story for a couple of reasons. First, powerful leading is, and has always been, a "full contact sport," requiring the best of those who wear its mantle. Bring yourself fully: *head* (thinking and rationale), *hands* (tactics and execution), *heart* (empathy and connectedness), and, as I'll argue later, *spirit* (connection to a purpose greater than yourself or your task). Bring it all, or don't bother. Parents, aching and weary from a brutal workday, call upon emotional stores they didn't know they could muster to share a tender moment, with spectacular presence, reading their children a bedtime story. Coaches, pounded by four consecutive losses and a rising tide of criticism in the local press, dig deep to not carry anger or frustration into the locker room when they prepare their teams to play with exactly the right game plan. Business leaders, required to keep one eye on the Wall Street ticker . . . well, you know how to complete this story. Bottom line, it's a challenging calling.

My second reason for telling this story is to point out that this stuff isn't new. Rather, it's in a very cluttered and confusing space. The volume of activity and results devoted to this topic is staggering. Search for "leadership" on Google and you'll discover more than 277,000 books written on the topic in the past forty years.

I suggest we start at the proper place for a very different dialogue about powerful leading, a place that gives all leaders at all levels some of the fundamentals that are overlooked or assumed in many of those 277,000 predecessors. I suggest we start with *you*. The journey to powerful leading always goes through the self. Always. To start with anything else is disingenuous and misleading. And to start with the self, I will provide a simple metaphor of the stream. Here we go:

I have a great store of natural passions, energies, and talents, from music and cooking to reading, teaching, and travel. I'm smart, energetic, and creative. Not only do these passions and talents provide me great joy and fulfillment, but I also perform best in life and leading others when all are completely available.

When I don't get the most out of whatever I am doing, including leading, I've found it is typically because there is something blocking this stream of natural energy, vitality, and passion.

What Is the Stream?

The stream is a central concept and powerful visual metaphor underlying my beliefs about guiding and developing leaders. As in the Wise Man parable, a clear, flowing stream represents a person's full engagement, possibility and performance. It's what brings you fulfillment and fires your talent. When your stream is clear, you are operating at full power and bringing everything that matters to you into your role as a leader. Your family life, spirituality, love for your work, zeal for physical health, whatever lets you burn hot without burning out—it's all relevant. You are tireless and inspiring, because when you are operating at peak potential, you empower others to do the same.

The stream has been a marvelous teaching aid for me, because it's such a visual idea. Try it now: imagine the stream running through the foothills that I talked about in the story you just read. Can you hear the trickling of the water, see the thriving reeds and water oaks, and watch the ducks and raccoons and fish that make their living from the water? There's an ecosystem that depends on you. It thrives when you are at your best and your stream of energy and honesty runs free and wild.

Experience has taught me that leaders lead best when they are authentic, energized and purposeful—aligned with who they are and what fires their souls. And here's the thing: nobody has to teach you a course in finding your stream! That's not a competency or skill. It's already a part of who you are. Most of the time, the simplest access each of us has to our full power as a leader is to discover and remove what's blocking our streams. It's simple "addition by subtraction." That is, the shortest distance between where most leaders operate and their full performance and potential is learning to remove obstacles that obstruct their streams, and sometimes even themselves!

What Blocks the Stream?

When we bring all of our humanity, intensity, presence, and mindfulness to the task of connecting with and leading others, we are authentic, powerful, and unstoppable. When we deny some of those components or fail to honor them, we create obstructions. Want to see the boulders that hold most leaders back? Here's a partial list in no particular order:

• *Lack of purpose.* We are never more powerful than when we are operating with a sense of purpose. You may recall a story about a man walking down a New York street who sees two bricklayers. One bricklayer is energized, working quickly and with clear relish. The other slogs, delays, and trudges through the same work.

Curious, the man asks the second bricklayer what he's doing and he replies, "Laying bricks, what do you think?" But when he asks the first, the bricklayer smiles and points to the sky, crowing, "Sir, I'm building a cathedral!" The same actions were motivated by a completely different sense of self-assigned purpose and as a result had a completely different energy source. Lack of connection to our core purpose is a great boulder in the center of many streams.

• *Poor self-care.* When we don't care for ourselves physically, mentally, emotionally, and spiritually, we will not have the energy to rise to challenges. It doesn't take a genius to know that many individuals in today's workplace put long hours before sleep, good nutrition, and mental balance. Noted author Jim Loehr likens the amount of energy required to succeed at leading in today's world to that of high-performance athletes and recommends we "train" similarly.

• *Self-limiting beliefs about others or ourselves*. My wife Cathy was, for years, a top external leadership trainer for Microsoft, but for a time she held a self-limiting and false belief that she was incapable of working effectively with C-suite executives. Only when she realized the folly and limitations in her thinking was she able to play fully at a higher level of her abilities. When we say, "I'm just a . . . ," we immediately limit our abilities to use what's in our streams. Fear-based or inaccurate thoughts are excuses for powerlessness.

• *Habits*. I know that in order to be the most effective person I can be, I should get up in the morning and get quiet and grounded before the chaos of the day begins—listen to a little music, read, reflect, and perhaps meditate. Instead, on most days I walk right to my computer and hop into the black hole known as Outlook. Why do I do what I know makes me operate less fully and less powerfully? Because knowledge is not sufficient to change behavior. We need motivation. Our unconscious attachment to habits is a huge boulder that keeps us rooted in the past. My habits keep me out of mindfulness and connection with what I say I want—and I persist in them *even though I know they are holding me back*.

• *Fear*. Fear is one huge boulder with many forms. For example, what holds you back from what Brad Blanton called "radical honesty," the act of stating blunt, direct truths as a means of freeing yourself and others from the stress and imprisonment of lies or half-truths and "pulled punches"? Underneath their bluster or public face, many leaders fear inadequacy (I'm not good enough), vulnerability (someone is stronger, smarter, more able), separation (others will reject me or my leadership), or lovability (I'm unworthy of others' love and esteem). Regardless of form or pathology, that is, where the fear developed and why we still hold on to it, fear calls us to hesitate, play small, tiptoe—you name the behavior—and represents a clear obstacle to a full and free expression of our talents and passion. Facing our fears takes time and patience.

• *Pretense.* Pretense is the habit of self-deception, of denying reality about ourselves and others. We pretend things are different from what they are. Only when we face the truth about ourselves do we gain the power to change things; only when we face the truth about others can we empower them.

Any obstruction of the stream, small or large, causes disruption. You get accelerating water, turbulence, and a slowing down of your ability to perform on the job—a malaise that will be familiar to anyone who feels "burned out." I frequently hear statements like, "You know, I don't have the same passion for my work that I used to." A blocked stream indicates that you are limiting the aspects of yourself that you bring to your work—obstructing the flow of passion, wit, candor, love of community, or whatever else charges your batteries. The inevitable results are ennui, cynicism, and despair.

LEADERSH*T

Being unaware of, or refusing to acknowledge,
the importance of your stream and the ways in which
you have allowed obstructions to reduce its flow.

LEADING

Accepting the reality of the stream,
taking steps to figure out why it's blocked, and
allowing your natural flow of passion, knowledge,
and enthusiasm define how you lead.

The Impact of a Blocked Stream

In the first stage of the journey with the Wise Man, we saw the environment's dependence on its source through the powerful visual image of the blocked stream that supports an interconnected web of activity. In its fully flowing and healthy state, it was a spawning ground for fish that local children caught downstream. It was a hunting and drinking area for local wildlife. It nourished wild edible crops and watered the roots of great old trees. When the stream was blocked, life downstream went dormant or died. All streams eventually merge with others; a blockage in one area will hinder the flow farther along. Any stream's influence extends far beyond its own banks.

As a leader, your influence has a similar scope of influence. Who you are on the job carries a potent sense of implied permission for those you lead. Your state of being—the clarity or obstruction of your stream—tells others who you expect them to be far more powerfully than your words or actions ever could. If you arrive at your office fractured by lingering anxieties, tired from overwork or poor self-care, triggered or angry, or weighted down with apathy, the people "downstream" from you cannot help but be poisoned by whatever you are dumping into your stream. Honesty, courage, a willingness to take great risks to produce great innovations . . . they all wither because your stream does not nourish their ability to grow in yourself or in others.

When leaders bring clear streams to their jobs, the impact is galvanic. A great example involves a client and longtime friend, Paul Viviano, a CEO since age twenty-seven who today runs Alliance HealthCare Services, a highly profitable company that is the bellwether of its industry. When Paul took the helm of Alliance in 2003, the company's culture was sleepy at best and toxic at worst. In the three months prior to his arrival, Alliance's stock price plummeted from $14 per share to about $4, symbolic of the dramatic shifts in the industry. Over the next three or four years, Paul and his team did everything humanly possible to right the ship. Their efforts in the marketplace eventually stabilized the company externally. But the culture internally was still as it had been: dysfunctional. They were working hard and maintaining, but it was despite themselves. Eventually, Paul and I arrived at the same conclusion: the company's performance challenges were direct correlates of its culture, the perfect embodiment of a clogged stream. Survey after survey suggested that employee engagement was marginal, as were the satisfaction levels of internal customers. With only minor digging within the organization, we found many important things left unsaid and many agreed-upon falsehoods about everything from performance to strategic decisions. Candor was discouraged, and Paul was brave enough to admit that this lack of candor began with him.

Paul's stream was blocked, in my judgment, by his fear of the consequences to morale and workforce stability if he told the truth as he saw things. This led to an environment where things that needed to be said were not, and where candor appeared in indirect ways including sarcasm. True candor springs from the courage and humility to admit one's own errors—to be the stream from which everyone else draws sustenance—and then to tell necessary truths. When Paul faced this fact about himself, he responded by convening a meeting of the company's senior leaders and openly sharing his failures in creating the kind of company he believed they could become. He placed the blame for those failures on his own shoulders. The power of his truthful statements was palpable, and the impact of that one act was transformative. Clearing your stream not only instantly restores life to the landscape, but the floodwaters *change* the landscape itself. Nothing can remain the same. While he has had to model the behavior of candor countless times over the past year, it is changing the culture of secrecy and pretense in dramatic ways.

The Presumption of Brokenness

So much of our postmodern business landscape is littered with failed systems for creating sustainable leaders because of what I call the *presumption of brokenness*. In this traditional school of thought, leading is what you do. Therefore, if you're not getting breakthrough results, you need to be taught to *do differently*. That's why a multi-billion-dollar industry has sprung up to "bolt on" the tools and methodologies that are supposed to make you a better leader. You're broken and inadequate, the industry says. You need our Harvard class on leadership, our training on high-performance teaming, our Outward Bound course, our materials, and *then* you'll be the next Jack Welch. Just more leadersh*t, I say.

This approach, while it has produced some valuable ideas, is at its heart ineffective. It makes "leadership" into a commodity that can be sold and implanted. While some tools and systems can be useful in the process of organizational transformation, they are not what leading is about. You are not broken. I do not enter any relationship with the presumption of brokenness, as though there were something lacking in you that only I, in my brilliance, can provide. You already possess 90 percent of what it takes to lead.

Leading is not simply about what you do. Leading others powerfully is more about who you are. Therefore, discovering your ability to lead others to breakthrough results is not about grafting someone else's methodology onto your current set of skills. It's about clearing away everything that is preventing you from showing up each day at the office and leading with your full passion and sense of purpose.

Here's the point. Strip away your college degrees, professional titles, awards, family connections. Stand naked before the world. Who and what are you? Are you a person of honor? Knowledge? Love? Passion? Courage? Creativity? Faith? If you are not leading your organization based on those essential qualities, it is very difficult to lead effectively. For some people, clearing their streams is a matter of releasing and celebrating those qualities. Others may need a change of scenery. An executive with a passion for data and empirical research may not be an effective leader in advertising but may thrive in engineering or accounting. It is possible to become a breakthrough leader in the right circumstances. The trick is making those circumstances happen.

Clearing your stream is a method for uncovering the qualities that make you love what you do and enable you to ignite others' passion for greatness, then discovering or creating the environment that recognizes and rewards those qualities.

LEADERSH*T

The idea that all leaders are lacking or broken in some way that only a prescriptive program that "bolts on" a solution can repair.

LEADING

Fully understanding that you have everything you need to lead effectively . . . when you are able to get out of your own way and let your talents and abilities to shine through.

The Stream and Athletic Performance

My work with the UCLA women's gymnastics team in 2010 illustrates how opening one's eyes to and removing self-created blockages can have a dazzling impact on performance. In February 2010, after the team dropped a home meet to Stanford (a team they believe they should have beaten) and fell in the polls to a national ranking of ninth, Head Coach Valorie Kondos Field asked me to address the team. This program, composed of incredible athletes with world-caliber credentials, had won five previous NCAA championships under Coach Valorie Kondos Field, known to all as Miss Val. I'd begun working with Miss Val as an executive coach the previous year and had begun to learn the intricacies of college gymnastics. It didn't matter whether the loss was a result of the burden of expectations based on the team's historical success or the burden of their own expectations: this team was angry after that loss at home.

As I most often do, I gave the group a chance to say what was on their minds. They voiced frustrations, halting at first, and then in a torrent, mostly about things over which they had no control: worries about letting their teammates down if they made a mistake, a focus on beating the other team, the noise of the crowd, the UCLA legacy, and on and on. That self-imposed noise (I'll talk more about noise later) was blocking the flow of the things these women could control: their talent, passion for the sport, and diligent training.

Before our work together, even Miss Val, a gifted leader and coach, had been experiencing something akin to burnout. "I had been voted NACGC [National Association of College Gymnastics Coaches] coach of the year by my peers four times and experienced quite a bit of success," she says. "But I was sick and tired of listening to myself talk. I needed a personal, professional facelift."

With Valorie, I simply helped her reconnect to her stream—her talents, passion and purpose—and escape the mental loop in which she had trapped herself. "You allowed me to step outside myself and look at where I had been and have a vision of where I wanted to go," she says. "I got very clear in being able to think of my future journey as a leader. Before, my brain was on repeat: Every September the team came in, we trained, we went to meets, and all the rest. There was no inspiration. I sat in your office, having this surreal experience where I was outside my body and seeing all the traits I had at my disposal. I was able to shake them all out, polish them all up, and open a new chapter in my career."

With the team, I took a simpler tack. I knew that I had to empower them to clear their own streams; Miss Val (or any other coach, for that matter) couldn't do it for them.

When you are on the balance beam, a four-inch-wide platform for some of the most riskiest gymnastics skills possible, your thoughts are solely yours! Over the next eight weeks, up to and including the NCAA National Championship, I kept it simple when I spoke with them. "Close your eyes and think of a beautiful mountain meadow with a stream meandering through it," I said. "It's four or five feet deep, with cool, crisp water." Not a single person had trouble getting a clear mental image; that's one of the beautiful things about the stream. "Now, imagine your stream becoming slowly clogged. Hikers throw a branch into it, boulders roll into it, leaves pile up from upstream. The flow of water slows to a trickle." I explained that the stream was their talent, training, passion, and discipline. With clear streams, I said, they would clear a space in which their gymnastics could come out fully, with nothing held back. They shared the boulders in their own streams and we discussed how they could remove them.

Bless them, these incredible athletes were willing to do anything to help them return to the level at which they knew they should be performing, and they embraced this simple metaphor with zeal. They collectively redirected their thoughts and started talking about "the bubble," that distraction-free headspace they aspired to occupy at all times. At the next meet, they had their highest team score in five years. No kidding. Look it up. And they lost only one meet the rest of the season and won a sixth national championship. They were gracious enough to give me a national championship ring, which I wear proudly.

I don't believe for a second that I can take much credit for the team's stunning turnaround. Talent, coaching genius, preparation, and passion all won the day. But their story does illustrate that even though there may be many boulders in our streams, just pulling out some of the smaller stones can get things flowing freely and begin the process that rolls those great boulders loose. When that happens, the potential that we have always possessed finally meets an environment where it can be truly expressed, and great things can and do result.

Access Points

At the end of each chapter, in a section called "Access Points," I will provide some questions and some space to assist in your reflection on the previous discussion. In each of these sections, I will present some tough questions that aided in my development as a leader and in the journeys of those whom I have coached. If you'll consider them honestly, these may be some of the toughest questions you'll ever ask yourself. I call them "access points" because I found that reflecting on tough questions and discovering my truthful answers gave me real access to the deeper truths about my life and my leading. Each of those truths was critical in my growth and development as a person and a leader. I hope they serve you, too, in that way!

ACCESS POINTS

The Tale of the Stream

Questions I've asked myself and others in our journeys toward keeping our streams clear of unwanted garbage:

What's my energy level for life right now? For work?
If they are different from each other, why?

_____

_____

_____

_____

_____

When in my life have I "played full out" (i.e., didn't hold back, expressed myself fully)? When has it occurred and what were the conditions enabling it?

_____

_____

_____

_____

_____

What fears stand in the way of achieving my full potential? What can I do to clear them away?

_____

_____

_____

_____

_____

What habits stand in the way of achieving my full potential? What can I do to clear them away?

_____

_____

_____

_____

_____

What beliefs stand in the way of achieving my full potential?
What can I do to clear them away?

_____

_____

_____

_____

_____

In what ways does my willingness to play fully relate to how I lead
others?

_____

_____

_____

_____

If I did engage in my life more fully (or more often), what would
that make possible that isn't possible now?

_____

_____

_____

_____

What's the one "truth" about my gifts and talents that I believe about myself but that I hesitate to let others know about? What about it makes me hesitate? What's it covering?

_____

_____

_____

_____

_____

Who can I fully trust to support my journey?

_____

_____

_____

_____

A Final Thought

When my stream is clear and free flowing,
my energy and passion for life and leading
are vibrant and unstoppable.
I'd rather live there.

TWO

The Tale of the Skipping Stones

Forever—is composed of Nows—
—Emily Dickinson

*D*rizzle and gray clouds greeted us the morning after our first day on the road. Watery darkness slowly became dreary, dishwater dawn as I woke. We had shared a cozy rental cabin outside a small village, the Wise Man comfortable on the ancient couch by the fire, me tucked into a huge rough-hewn bed. He was up and about with his restless energy—rolling a cigarette, scraping mud off his ancient boots, standing in front of a mirror trimming his nose hairs with the precision of a sculptor working a piece of alabaster. I watched him do all this because I was sore: back, hamstrings, shoulders, knees. The long day on the trail (we had done an estimated nine miles, not bad for a deskbound character like me), plus removing the objects from the stream, had been quite a workout. I prayed that coffee and ibuprofen were in my immediate future.

"Up," he said. He rolled the covers off me, the cruel

bastard. "*You'll feel better once we get moving. You're gonna like where we're going today.*" *A thumb cocked toward the hot plate in the corner.* "*Made some coffee.*"

Bless you, I thought. Groaning, I pulled on my clothes and poured myself a large cup of low-grade jet fuel: Greek-style coffee, syrupy and strong. Synapses began to fire in my brain and I felt my muscles loosen a bit. The previous day had been a pleasure, despite my aches. I felt grateful to be where I was, when I was, with this companion, not knowing what was to come next. It struck me that one of the great blessings of being outside the well-worn floorboards of one's familiar routine was not knowing what lay around the next corner. I couldn't plan or predict. I had to be in the present moment and respond. Ignorance, I decided as I surveyed the dripping, sodden landscape outside the window, was bliss.

The March Downstream

"*Okay, Professor, let's get moving.*"

My companion (who had taken to calling me Professor after he found out that I had a doctoral degree) was merciless. I laced up my boots, brushed my teeth, hoisted my pack onto my sore shoulders, and followed my guide out the door into the growing daylight. He gave me a wink and, without a word, headed off at his usual brisk clip along the fire road that led from our cabin and down a sloping side trail. Trees crowded around us for at least a half hour, but when they began to thin I saw a familiar landscape and realized that we were backtracking: retracing our steps back to the stream that we had unblocked just the day before.

The Wise Man turned off the trail and began bush-whacking downstream just as he had upstream to the blockage that had choked the flow of water. It was slow-going and, as the day warmed up, hot work. Sweat flowed and I stopped to strip off layers. My companion, unflappable, never paused or seemed to overheat.

Finally, however, he seemed to sense my doubt about our route. "There was an old trail up here, if I remember correctly," he said over his shoulder. "Once we hit that, we'll be home free all the way down to her, don't you worry."

"Down to what?"

He turned to look back and shot me a smile with raised eyebrows, then marched on. After another half hour of hacking and high-stepping our way through nettles and pools of standing water, I was sure that my companion's memory had failed when he shot out a sudden "Ha!" and I knew he had found his trail. What I stepped onto about ten seconds later was really the echo of a trail, an overgrown track the width of my forearm and studded with wild lettuce and dandelions. But it was straight and flat. Without a word, he doubled his pace and I fell in behind him, heading downstream.

I couldn't help but wonder who the "her" was that we headed for. As we clicked into a hiking rhythm, the soundscape around us grew rich and varied: the chuckle of flowing water, the whisper of a breeze in the tall grass, and the occasional punctuation of a bird's call, all set to the rhythm of our boots thudding on the packed dirt. It was hypnotic.

Another hour, three more miles. We were walking nearly shoulder-to-shoulder, not speaking, when we abruptly turned a sharp bend in the trail. I stopped dead. "There she is," said my companion. Before us lay a shimmering, utterly calm pond at least a quarter-mile across and just as broad, wisps of mist still curling from its center. Bordered on all sides by trees, it was like a cool, shaded hole in the deep green felt of the landscape. Not a ripple broke its gray-green surface. It was profoundly quiet—no chattering ducks, jumping fish or children swinging out on a rope ladder to cannonball into the water. It felt like a place no human had been for many years.

Past, Present and Future

The Wise Man inhaled deeply. He felt it, too. "Come on," he said. The trail wound along the west edge of the pond and led us to a scattering of large flat stones, some as big as office desks, which had doubtless been used over the years as picnic tables or meditation seats by visitors. We sat down on one, glad to be off our feet and enjoying the borrowed warmth of the rock. Neither of us spoke for a while; it would have seemed sacrilegious.

"This is what our stream feeds, in part," he said. He swept his arm over the expanse of the pond. "But there's a fundamental difference between the stream and this, and that's why I wanted to bring you here. Plus, down that way about four miles is a town with a great Irish pub, and I would sell one of my kidneys for a beer right about now."

I had to laugh at that. "What's the fundamental difference?"

"Think about it, Professor. They're made of the same substance, good old H_2O. Water is water whether it's flowing in the creek or pooling in this pond. But the water in the stream is always in motion. Its nature is to move toward the future. It is physically impossible for it to come to rest. It can't until it becomes part of a larger body like this one, and then it's no longer a stream."

He waved his arm over the pond. "The pond," he continued, "is the opposite. Its water is locked up and stationary. A lake or pond is forever in the moment with nowhere to go but now." The echo of his voice sank into the water, and I savored its meaning. It was a wonderful metaphor for the duality of human nature.

My turn. "So each of us is forever in motion, but also confronted by times when we're required by circumstance to be completely present in the moment, like the water that has no choice but to flow into the lake," I said.

He nodded like a teacher to a pupil who's aced a tough question. "Not bad." He stooped to heft a smooth oval stone. "Think about the water as human perception," he went on. "Even a quiet pond has outlet streams where the water flows away from it.

We're the same way. Even when we're fully present in the moment, we continue to move into the future. We go from the stream of the past to the stream of the future through the lake of the present, one moment at a time. We're simultaneously in the present moment and flowing toward the future. It's being aware of that duality and doing something with it that great leaders do."

Skipping Stones

He cocked his wrist, and with a curious sidearm motion and a twist of the hip, he flung the stone out across the glassy surface of the pond. It hit and skipped. One, two, three, four, five, six, seven, eight, nine times before its momentum died and it sank into the pool. The motion had looked effortless, but the stone had traveled at least seventy yards.

"Wow," I said. "Nice. You play baseball as a kid?"

"A little. Baseball, football, hockey—pretty much everything." He bent again and grabbed two stones, handing *me one. It was a near-perfect oval, about four inches long, made to fit into a grown man's hand. "You ever skip stones as a kid?"*

"Of course," I replied. "Who didn't?"

He tapped my stone with his finger. "Then you know the secrets to being a successful skipper, and I don't mean of the Gilligan's Island *variety."*

That was my cue to give it a try. Trying to find my footing on the damp grass, I felt like a rookie pitcher coming in to relieve Sandy Koufax. I hoped I could get my stone to skip four times just to avoid making an ass of myself. I rocked, pulled my left leg back in my best Nuke LaLoosh impression, and with a sidearm flick of my wrist sailed my stone into space. Skip, skip, skip, sink. Survey says . . . ass.

The Wise Man threw back his head and roared with laughter at what must have been the embarrassed expression on my face. The sound rolled and reverberated around the pond until I caught the fever and started laughing right along with him. We howled until our heads and jaws ached, perhaps bringing this hushed corner of the world the loudest disturbance it had known in years.

Eventually, we got ourselves under control. "A game effort, Professor," my guide said. "You looked like a flamingo trying yoga for the first time." Another chuckle. "I think it's one of the great pearls of wisdom that it takes many years of relentless work and effort to make something look effortless, whether it's skipping a stone across water or wrestling the 'monkey mind' to be in the present."

He grabbed another stone and went on. "The skipping stone is a beautiful metaphor for the mental state that a great leader needs to have. Think about it: as a culture, we value motion above all else. A successful person is the one who's constantly on the go, working long hours, doing more than the other guy. When we talk about great businesspeople, we compare them to sharks, which drown if they stop moving. Right?"

"I've used that comparison myself," I said.

"Sure you have. It's the accepted wisdom," he replied. "But what if it's wrong? What if we're all like the skipping stones?" To prove his point, he bent and picked up another perfect stone, which wind and water seemed to have carved intentionally to be thrown. He handed it to me. I hesitated, then took it.

"You going to laugh at me?"

His eyes glittered. "Probably. Go ahead, but relax this time. Less leg kick, a smoother motion with your arm, and a strong flick of the wrist at the end." I nodded, rocked, and with a flick of my wrist, flung my stone. Six skips and then plunk, into the drink. Perhaps things were not hopeless after all.

"Excellent!" the Wise Man crowed. "Much better. But think now about the stone. As long as it's in motion, it *skips along the surface—the barest fraction of an inch—of water that must be fifty, sixty feet deep. It doesn't even get completely wet. Not until it exhausts that borrowed kinetic energy and sinks into the pond does it slowly settle, arcing back and forth as it sinks to the bottom, to become a part of the deeper whole. When we're moving at top speed, all we experience is a few centimeters of surface. A good, wise leader settles into the moment. That's the place where true leading lives."*

Motion and Stillness

I stared out at the pond as the sun moved past noon; the day had grown warm and breezy. I tried to imagine the stone I had thrown turning and wavering as it dropped to a dappled green bottom. In seconds, it had gone from a frenetic jumping trajectory to dimly lit, motionless peace. My companion motioned for me to follow him, and we made our way back to our flat stone seats, where we opened our packs and ate lunch. Trail mix and water. I sighed. Exchanging one of my limbs for a couple of cold ones was starting to look like a pretty reasonable transaction.

After a few minutes, he said, "A fully functional person—a fully effective leader—needs to be both aspects of the skipping stone. You need to skip along the surface because that's motion, energy, and direction. It gets you somewhere."

"But you also need to be the settling stone," I interrupted

through a mouthful of nuts and raisins. "Stop moving and sink into the present, when you can be mindful of everything going on around you and everyone who's a part of what you're doing."

He nodded. "The best are both, all the time, at the same time. It's a difficult balance, but great leaders manage to maintain it."

I blew out a great puff of air. It seemed nearly impossible to be rapidly moving forward, skimming the surface of events and relationships, and to simultaneously maintain a cool, settled center in each moment. At my best, I could bring myself into fleeting mindfulness, with great effort, only to let the first distraction pull me into the stream of past and future.

Finally I said, "But how do you get there? How can you be both at the same time?"

The Wise Man stood, brushed off his pants, and picked his way back to the lakeshore. Knowing what he would do, I tailed him, then stooped and hefted an oblong stone from the ground and tossed it to him. "Tools of the trade," I said.

He smiled and then eyed the surface of the water with one eye closed, shifted his weight, whipped his right arm around and zing! At least seventeen skips before I lost count, an arrow of rippled water spreading from each impact until the rock vanished. He clapped his hands and then turned to me.

"The same way you get to skip a stone twenty times on a forest pond, Professor," he said. "Lots and lots of practice." He trudged back to our stone table and began stuffing things into his pack. We were skipping like stones on this trail excursion, moving from shelter to shelter over the miles. But were we also settling into a series of moments? I felt more open to meanings, not just appearances. Perhaps this was practice. Practice makes perfect, right?

"You coming?" He was loaded and ready for the trail and had kindly reassembled my pack as well.

"Yeah," I said. I didn't move. I was staring at the lake, trees, and sky and didn't want to break the mood.

"Well, come on then." The sound of his footsteps told me he had already begun to head for the trail. "We've got another two hours or so. First round's on me."

In the afternoon heat, a few beers in a cool pub over deep conversation sounded like heaven. I crouched to grab a small, perfect throwing stone and let it slide into my pocket, then grabbed my pack and trotted to catch up with my companion, who was already headed for the tree line and the shade.

My Thoughts on The Tale of the Skipping Stones

In this section, I'll speak to the idea that leading begins with, and is made possible by your presence—a state of being in which you fully experience the moment you are living in. Said another way, it's impossible to lead when you're not in the room. I'll share some of the primary barriers to presence, our tendency to live in the past or future instead of the present, provide thoughts on the difference between being and doing in effective leadership, and discuss the meaning of the performance moment.

Peter Drucker, a diminutive Austrian who was one of the most eminent management theorists of the twentieth century, was known to emphatically proclaim in his lectures, "Mr. Manager, you must MAN-AGE!" My rant is similar for leaders. "Mr. or Ms. Leader, you must SHOW UP!" To me, that's central to any discussion of powerful lead-ing. Simply put, showing up means being present and in the room—unencumbered by your worries, fears, projections, and judgments—so you can be at your best and help others to do the same. This chapter will explore how that simple act of being present, in the boardroom and on the playing field, relates to creating optimal results.

Ellen Langer, the esteemed social psychologist who coined the term *mindfulness* to translate an ancient Buddhist concept into modern terms, made a critically important distinction between the ideas of mindfulness and *presence*. This distinction is vital as we strive to understand the qualities that a great leader possesses. To Langer and others, *presence* is being awake, aware and conscious in the moment. One of the traits that make us human is our minds' ability to extend our thoughts back to relive experiences in the past or forward to anticipate or predict the future. It's a wonderful gift, and we often give in to the temptation to spend most of our psychological lives in the past and future, regretting what cannot be changed or worrying about what we have yet to do. The result is that we are rarely in the now, fully present in life as it is happening.

ISDOM LEADING CONCEPTS

- Showing up powerfully as a leader first means being mindfully present

- A leader's mindful presence has the power to create breakthrough results

- For one's optimal athletic performance, presence is everything

- Conventional leadership theory claims that great leading is about what you are doing, while my evidence states that the most powerful leading involves "who you are being"

ISDOM LEADING GOALS

- Understanding mindful presence and being able to identify when you are present and when you are not

- Assessing how often you "show up" powerfully for your people

- Focusing more on who you are being than on simply "getting shit done"

- Being hyper-aware of performance moments and being a great leader when they arise

- Developing the tools to become more mindfully present

It is only when we are completely present in the moment that we are capable of fully experiencing everything it contains: intentions, implications, and fine details of sight and sound that otherwise vanish into the rush of living.

As I have explained to many of my coaching clients over the years, presence is not enough for a leader who aspires to produce breakthrough performance. One of my core beliefs about leading states that transformation can only happen in others when that individual leader has passed beyond mere presence to *mindfulness*. To be mindful is to be present while also being fully aware of how

---

LEADERSH*T

Letting your thoughts dwell on the unchangeable past
or the unknowable future when you're supposed to
be in the present with your people.

LEADING

Resisting the temptation to dwell on past or future but being
mindfully present, both living in the moment and aware of
how and why you react to what occurs in each moment.

---

your assumptions, beliefs, and biases are shaping your responses to everyone and everything in real time. It's being hyper-aware of your mental models, maps, and patterns even as you are speaking and reacting to what other people do and say.

If you're saying to yourself that mindfulness is a pretty advanced state, you're right. However, I coach executives in developing mindful presence quite regularly, and it's within reach of nearly anyone with the self-awareness and discipline to seek it. Mindful presence is at the core of my work. As anyone who has worked with me can tell you, one of my favorite phrases is that "leading is about *how you show up.*" You can't lead if you're not mentally in the room.

How Are You Showing Up?

Showing up fully is the most important aspect of being an effective leader. Showing up means being in the now. It means being fully cognizant of all the stimuli that come from the people and situations you encounter. As you consciously evolve into a more capable leader, you'll strip away all the things that prevent you from showing up fully and mindfully.

In the modern world, where our value is largely an outgrowth of how much and how fast we take action, there's an endless litany of things that can pull our minds away from the moment:

- Regret over things done in the past
- Worries about what might happen in the future
- Fear about our ability to cope with the demands before us
- Mental "junk food" that pulls our minds from the present, from e-mail to text messages
- Boredom that encourages the mind to wander
- The demands of "urgent" affairs that are not so urgent

In the parable of the skipping stones, I made the point that being mindful and present, settling into oneself in a situation, is the only way to partake of the whole of that situation. When the skipped stone stops and sinks, it becomes part of the lake and is affected by that new environment. Warren Bennis said, "The leader and the led are intimate allies." Leading others most often means being fully present and aware so that you can be critically and sensitively aware of moods, emotions and thoughts—both your own and others'.

Imagine an orchestral conductor like Esa-Pekka Salonen of the Los Angeles Philharmonic. Could a world-class conductor show up for a performance of Beethoven's Ninth anything but fully present and mindful and hope for success? Of course not. Not only does he have to be completely present in order to take in the shadings of the performance as it unfolds, but he must also be mindful. If a few of the violas are not at their best on a given evening, he must be aware of it to make spontaneous changes based on his experience and skill.

Truly showing up and settling into yourself grants you incredible power to manage and optimize a situation or a team, because you become the conductor. Your followers are your violins, oboes and percussion. You become more aware of what people want, fear, and are capable of in the moment. As the leader, you set the cues for everyone. The more mindful and aware you are, the more others will be as well.

Contrast two styles of leading: I have attended business meetings that seethed with the tension you might find in a room of people assembled to watch a lethal injection. In one case, the creative director of an advertising agency would assemble his people every week for a meeting that was ostensibly about creative work but was really about slapping wrists, rehashing arguments, and making dire predictions about revenues if the team didn't "shape up." No one was really present for these egotistical interrogations; they were wishing to be somewhere else. This ad agency turned over 50 percent of its personnel each year, at a staggering cost.

On the opposite end was a Texas-based small publisher. This company, which had come to redefine its industry, was a model of independence and entrepreneurship. The founder and CEO was continually present with his people, assessing the autonomy and expertise of each of his editors and marketers and giving them the freedom to express their own vision in crafting their segment of the business. The sense of ownership in the employees was extraordinary because the company's leader recognized their individual styles and let them express those, only stepping in when course correction was needed.

Mindful Presence on the Softball Diamond

I witnessed the impact of this core principle when I worked with Kelly Inouye-Perez, head coach of the UCLA softball team, and her players in 2010. I'll talk more about Kelly and my experience with her team later, but suffice it to say here that she had been under crippling pressure from the community when I met with her. But at the NCAA Women's College World Series (WCWS), she told me that she put the concept of mindful presence to work from the moment the team bus rolled into ASA Hall of Fame Complex in Oklahoma City.

In previous seasons, she'd had a difficult time tuning out the crowd and other distractions (like a national television audience and interviews by ESPN's Holly Rowe between innings) so she could focus on her players and the pitch-by-pitch action of the game. Not in 2010. With some coaching from me, Kelly had disciplined her mind so that she was able to be incredibly present for her players at each pitch, completely mindful of how she and her players were was feeling and reacting. Her mindful presence gave her the ability to *monitor* the mental and emotional states of each player on the field and in the dugout. This empowered her to optimize the results that each player could deliver according to her ability.

LEADERSH*T
Falling prey to distractions and fears
so that you cannot be present for your people.

LEADING
Noticing, then releasing, those same distractions
so that you can monitor your followers
to ensure they have what they need
to function at their peak.

Kelly's complete presence in the 2010 postseason, culminating at the Women's College World Series, gave her players the confidence that she had their backs. It also inspired them to engage their own mindful presence during every at-bat and while in the field. They embraced their coach's inner calm and were able to "slow the game down," a phrase that became their motto during the season. They responded to events consciously rather than reacting reflexively and without thinking. I don't think it will surprise you that UCLA went 10-0 in the 2010 postseason, including at the Women's College World Series, sweeping eight-time champion Arizona 2-0 in the best-of-three final series. It was UCLA's twelfth national title and Kelly's first as head coach.

Human Being Versus "Human Doing"

I have said that our culture devalues living in it. Dig deeper and you'll find a society that rewards *doing* over *being*—gives the currency of action greater value than the currency of presence and perspective. It's the skipping of the stones—the endless, frenetic motion that captures our attention even though it's basically shallow—that garners all the praise, not the settling of that same stone. Some people brag about how little sleep they get and how many hours they put in per week. We're human beings, but we could plausibly rename ourselves "human doings" based on what our world cherishes most.

I watched a piece on the CBS program *Sunday Morning* called "The Art of the Obituary," and in it, obit writers described how few surviving family members, when interviewed about the deceased, said anything about the deceased's work. We take such pride in what we do, but all these family members could talk about was what their loved ones *gave*—as parents, spouses, church members, leaders in the community, and so on. We give our time and energy to that which expresses who we are, not what we do. That's what moves others.

Getting Shit Done (GSD)

Unfortunately, "being" over "doing" is a tough sell to executives. I'm not suggesting for a moment that running a corporation can be all calm navel contemplation. Effectively leading a team or organization in today's crazy world will always demand hard work, commitment to do what must be done, alignment of purpose, and brilliant execution. Our current model is to act fast; mindfulness feels like a luxury. But mindful presence and its connection with who we are should both *precede* and *determine* the actions that leaders take. Mindful presence should be as elemental for leaders as breathing.

Instead, business is crowded with executives who are known for GSD: Getting Shit Done. They fancy themselves to be take-no-prisoners operators with a copy of Sun Tzu's *Art of War* in their suit pocket. But in reality, they are often bundles of triggers and reactions moving from one setting to another. Rather than bringing their best to a situation, they bring ego and judgment along with action. They are merely problem solving, not bringing out the brilliance in others. They might get things done, but technical competence is not what this book is about, nor will it build and unleash the genius of others.

An unspoken compact in our civilization allows GSD leaders to thrive. Unless we consciously opt out (and it takes effort and will to do so), we all live, to some degree, in the nanosecond. I do it myself. I get upset if it takes more than one second to send an e-mail. We want what we want as soon as we think of it. As a result, we are not a mindfully present society. We even set up laws to force ourselves to be more present, such as those banning texting while driving. We know that we need to come back to the moment; we just can't seem to manage it.

Insidious company conference calls are a great example of "doing" pressure. They are scheduled on the hour, for an hour; fifty minutes in, our minds are no longer on that call. We're thinking about disengaging the first and getting to the next one. When you finish call number one and dial, late, into call number two, can you shift gears right away? No. You're dwelling on what actions you committed to in the last call—and what you'll talk about in the next call. We check out of the present moment and leave no forwarding address. Our brains were not designed for this. There's nothing left when we're called to examine our reactions, observe our patterns, or assess what other people need to be their best.

LEADERSH*T

Expecting instant gratification and focusing on
incessant but meaningless activity
because you feel that your activities define you.

LEADING

Allowing your mind to quiet down into
a state of motionlessness,
and simply being who you are capable of being.

Performance Moments

I call those instances *performance moments.* I borrowed the idea from years of working with athletes, especially at the collegiate level, and adapting their methods of evoking winning performance to business. Performance moments are where the theory of mindful presence meets the practical reality of leading people to breakthrough results.

Athletes in any sport know exactly what a performance moment is. It's that moment when everything is on the line: the key at-bat with the tying runs on base, the putt in the final-round playoff, the down-by-one free throw with no time left. In those situations, winning athletes will talk about being "in the zone," when the game seems to slow and the ball looks huge. That's mindful presence. They are not thinking about their failed at-bat or their missed three-point shot. They aren't worrying about what the press will write if they strike out. Mind, body, and spirit are completely in the moment, immersed in it and detached from it at the same time, analyzing every detail, aware of every muscle. There's no place for fear or doubt.

Athletes who can put themselves in that state of perfect calm, balance, and awareness do great things. Michael Jordan was able to do it for most of his career. He wasn't always the greatest ball handler or outside shooter in the game, but he had that rare ability to tune out the screaming crowd and crushing pressure and bring his "A" game when the championship was on the line. It's mental discipline, not speed or strength, that separates the champions from other elite athletes.

Some athletes are less successful at this. They give in to the "tyranny of expectations." They imagine what others expect or demand from them, what's on the line, and what will happen if they can't deliver. So they don't deliver. They "choke." For example, if you're a college basketball fan, you'll recall the infamous non-timeout called by Chris Webber of the Michigan Wolverines during the 1993 NCAA basketball finals. With twenty seconds left to play and his team down by two, Webber called a timeout. Smart—except that his team didn't have any timeouts left. That earned Michigan a technical foul and North Carolina a free throw. Game over.

I don't know what Webber's mindset was at that moment, but he was a twenty-year-old kid and obviously rattled. Following the game, he forgot the combination to his locker, accidentally tossed his wallet in the trash, and walked around the locker room with shaving cream on his ear. It's not a stretch to believe that he felt the pressure of the game, lost the moment, and panicked.

For a leader in business, a performance moment is that split second when you're on the cusp of choosing how you will engage someone you are leading—a teachable moment. On one hand, you can give in to the moment and the pressures you're feeling. On the other, you can serve your duty as a leader: to help that individual build capacity to create breakthrough results. Your choice determines whether you hit the ball out of the park or strike out.

Leading is performing in those small moments when the spotlight is off. Powerful leading happens when you've just gotten off four hours of high-stress phone calls, your e-mail inbox is about to explode, you have an angry voice mail from a board member . . . and your assistant says, "Boss, got a minute?" That's a performance moment.

There's a stanza in poet Oriah Mountain Dreamer's "The Invitation" that expresses this idea beautifully:

> It doesn't interest me
> to know where you live
> or how much money you have.
> I want to know if you can get up
> after the night of grief and despair
> weary and bruised to the bone
> and do what needs to be done
> to feed the children.

Your job is, literally, to make your employees great. Do you give in to your immediate need to be left alone, squeeze that anger trigger, and bite her head off? Or do you show up big, remembering your commitment to lead, humble yourself, slow or dial back your reaction, and listen? Showing up in that moment tells her that you respect what she brings to the table—that she is important. Home run with the bases loaded in the bottom of the ninth.

LEADERSH*T

Reacting to the need of a follower based on your own
stress, fear, frustration, or exhaustion.

LEADING

Understanding that your main job as a leader is
to make your followers great and being fully present
for people in the moment when they need you to be.

Those moments might come a hundred times in a single day. If you're a parent, they might come a thousand times in a day. That's why truly great leaders are not easy to find. Leading (or parenting) brilliantly is *hard work*.

Becoming Mindfully Present

So how can we, as leaders, put ourselves in position to triumph in those performance moments? How can we get ourselves, if not in a state of mindful presence 24-7, able to slip into that state of being when the need calls for it and really come through for our people when they look to us?

As I wrote in the Introduction to this book, after thirty years of observing the best leaders and athletes, I can say with confidence that the quickest way to improve performance is to strip away the things that get in the way of us being mindfully present. We clear away the clutter that prevents full expression.

One of the best and simplest access points to mindful presence is breathing. Examine your breath right now. Odds are your breathing was shallow until I called your attention to it, and then you took a deep inhale. It's amazing how poorly we breathe during the work-day. The overused word *inspiration* literally means, "to breathe." The Buddha said that breath is the access to consciousness. You begin to gain greater access to mindful presence through deep breathing. It clears the mind and makes you more aware of sensory input and your physical and mental state. A C-level executive once revealed to me in conversation that he was not aware of his breathing through-out his entire workday, which commonly ran to a punishing sixteen hours. When he was conscious of his breathing, he was calmer and clearer. Now aware, he began a new practice. When he started work at seven in the morning, he would close his door, close his eyes, and breathe deeply for ten minutes. He was calmer, more present, and more able to access his talents and wisdom.

Simply being silent, shutting down the flow of words and information that accompany our ceaseless motion, works wonders as well. We are not wired for silence; we suffer from the "monkey mind," that spastic, jittery consciousness that jumps from branch to branch without lingering on any thought for more than a split second. Yet silence allows us to settle into who we are in the moment. There is prodigious power in silence. All successful athletes know this. In business, we need to play catch-up.

Some time ago, I watched as a colleague introduced this concept to the leaders of DaVita, a progressive, wildly successful, and hyper-paced healthcare services client. She asked them to sit for thirty seconds of silence. It was agony. But by day four of this same meeting, they were up to five minutes of silence. The hardest, most skeptical of the bunch said, "This was a breakthrough for me." Now she starts all her meetings with a "three-minute sit" where everyone sits quietly and settles in. Silence gives each person the opportunity to breathe, consider and discard nonproductive thoughts of the past or future, relax and focus, and become fully present. The organization has improved its effectiveness just by doing that—by doing *nothing*.

You have what you need to lead. No book will make you smarter or more decisive. Rather, I've observed that the shortest path to breakthroughs comes from getting out of your own way. You don't have to show up at work acting like Yoda. But try walking down the hall more slowly. Breathe. Say hello to people. Slow down. Give yourself the time and space to settle in and see what you are capable of. Connect with your joys, passion, and vision for something better. Practice settling in; see what you and all those around you are capable of. It will amaze you.

ACCESS POINTS

The Tale of the Skipping Stones

Questions I've asked myself and others in our journeys to greater mindfulness and presence:

In any moment, am I skimming over the surface or settling in like the stone?

_____

_____

_____

_____

_____

What's my typical state of presence during a typical day? How do I know?

_____

_____

_____

_____

_____

When I am surface skimming, especially in interactions with others, what's the emotion or reality I'm hiding from?

_____

_____

_____

_____

_____

When do I feel most alive and present?

_____

_____

_____

_____

When I feel alive and present, what impact does that have on me? Those around me? My goals and sense of what I'm capable of achieving?

_____

_____

_____

_____

_____

If presence is mindful, what "addictions" (e.g., e-mail, phone) keep me *mind-less?*

_____

_____

_____

_____

_____

How do I (or others) recognize it when I am not present, when I am *mind-less?*

_____

_____

_____

_____

_____

When I am in full GSD mode, reacting instantly to stimuli coming my way, how fully am I showing up for myself? My team? My family?

_____

_____

_____

_____

_____

What are the consequences to me, my team, and my family if my GSD (a.k.a. mind-less) behavior doesn't change in one year? Five years? Ten years?

_____

_____

_____

_____

_____

What's one simple act or ritual I can engage in that returns me to greater presence and awareness?

_____

_____

_____

_____

_____

A Final Thought

For me, an extremely worthy goal in life
is to master the simple act of living in it.

THREE

The Tale of the Empty House

Meanings are not determined by situations,
but we determine ourselves by the meanings we give to situations.
—Alfred Adler, Austrian psychiatrist

he morning dawned hot and fine as we began our third day together. Setting out from the village where we had talked with colorful locals late into the night, we skirted a swampy stretch of ground and ascended a series of switchbacks that made the early hours hard going.

As always, the Wise Man seemed unaffected by the hill climbing; I couldn't tell whether he was exceptionally fit, unperturbed by the exertion, or a little of both. I felt the dust and the heat and drank copious amounts of water as we doubled back, left then right, gamely navigating what must have been at least 700 feet of elevation gain. Obviously, we were climbing out of the valley cut by the river we had cleared and heading for high ground. My quads and calves ached at the prospect of a day of climbing, descending, and then climbing some more.

But when my companion, who was some fifty yards ahead of me by ten o'clock, crested the final rise and stood on top of this endless hill, he let out a yawp like something out of a Walt Whitman poem, then with a wide grin doffed his hat and wiped his brow. I hustled to catch up with him. At the top, this what I saw: not a march of more hot and dusty climbs but a landscape of farms and fields dotting the countryside with the neat green geometry of crop rows, huge rolls of fresh hay grass, and rows of split-rail fences. Into the distance meandered a dirt road that was blessedly flat and dotted with shade-giving elms, willows, and peach trees.

I could have sworn I heard my knees give a quiet prayer of thanks.

"How about that, Professor?" The Wise Man was tipping back his own water bottle and waving at the beckoning landscape as though he had created it.

He hefted his pack and I did the same. "Let's put some miles behind us," he said. We walked the road enveloped in the smells of manure, damp straw, sawdust, and alfalfa. Cruising past small farms and ranches—perhaps ten acres at most, many much smaller—the road was a hiker's delight: level, soft dirt with banked turns. It was almost absurdly bucolic country, and I found myself wondering what kind of backbreaking work went into creating the scene of serenity that I glimpsed in passing.

The House in the Field

Devouring the miles with long strides, we passed by dairy farms and orchards, stables, and vineyards laden with grapes. Eventually, as we turned a corner, the rutted road became asphalt and we walked into the two-block downtown of a tiny, one-stoplight hamlet. Other than the flies buzzing in the noontime heat, the town center was still and deserted; this was a workday and there was much to be done.

We stopped over at a general store to pick up cold drinks and supplies, then asked the clerk to suggest the most scenic path out of town. The tall, lanky fellow with a prominent Adam's apple said simply, "State Route 112, that way," pointing at the four-way intersection we'd just walked through. "Take it for about a mile, and then you'll see a branching trail on the right. Take the left fork down the hill, not the right fork. You don't want to go that way. The haunted house is that way." Then he tipped his cap to us and turned away.

The Wise Man's eyes met mine and we shared the same thought. Haunted house? Oh, there was no way we were passing that up. We thanked our guide, ducked out the door and headed up the state road out of the tiny town. After about twenty minutes' walking, we found the clearly marked trail beside the road. It was wide and well maintained, and it indeed forked after a quarter mile. I was reminded of a Robert Frost poem: the left way was well-trodden and pocked with boot prints and led down a gentle grade to a ridge above a valley. The right was overgrown with grass and had clearly seen little foot traffic. The haunted house lay that way, and my companion and I shot each other a smile. Then he strode off and we took the road less traveled by.

Haunted houses can come in all shapes and sizes; in my experience, they rarely live up to the hype. Odds were we were headed for a rotted-out barn or maybe the ruined stone foundation of a farmstead where some drunk highschoolers swore they'd seen the ghost of a former teacher. I didn't expect much more. After hours on the trail, the anticipation of the unknown was enough.

So it was with stunned admiration that we passed a thick stand of poplar trees smothered in ivy and saw an ornate, decrepit, gorgeous grande dame of a Victorian mansion sitting on its own in the middle of a field of witch grass and dandelions. Both of us stopped dead; this was not a house, but a house.

It was at least a century old, wrought with gables and cupolas and fussy gingerbread trim and massive wooden pillars that looked like the mainmasts of square-rigged schooners. The building had long ago shed its paint under the assault of wind, rain, and sun, but it possessed a grandeur and dignity that had nothing to do with color or surroundings. This was a house sure to be filled with stories.

Visitors in the Night

"Wow, this is a time machine, to be sure," the Wise Man said, stroking his beard and staring up at the magnificent old structure. He set his pack on the ground and started slowly circling the property as if appraising it. I followed him and took in the scene: the peeling paint and broken screens of a vast enclosed porch on the west side; a teetering balcony off what must have been the master bedroom on the back, facing south toward the distant mountains; a stone pond long dried up; a gorgeously carved side entrance (a servants' entrance, most likely) with steep stairs and a gazebo-like foyer.

"This place is a work of art," I finally whispered as we came back around to the front of the mansion. "It's got to date back to, what, the Gilded Age?"

"I'd say so, and it would make sense. This was rail baron country—not too far from the commercial centers and the coal regions, but far enough for a stately country retreat." His eyes fixed on the front door. "I wonder what happened here?"

It was a leading question, and though I knew it, I couldn't help but be fascinated with this stunning home. Even after decades, all the windows were intact. The walls had not been torn into for their copper pipes and wiring, both of which would bring a pretty price. There were stone statues and marble decorations on the grounds, both of which locals should have spirited away years before for their own living gardens. Yet this place appeared relatively untouched by time. Why?

"One way to find out," I said, and headed for the wide, curving steps up to the front door. Conscious of the distance to medical help, I tested the first step with my weight. Not a creak. The second was solid, as was the third. Okay, in for a penny, in for a pound, I thought. I climbed the steps to the porch and tried the tarnished knob on the front door. It turned and the door, sticking and cracking slightly after swelling from years of humidity, swung open. I was about to enter when I heard a sound behind me and there was my companion, who'd climbed the front steps cat-quietly and was as eager as I was to get a look inside the old place.

I expected the reek of mold, piles of ancient draperies, and dust outlines marking where Chippendale furnishings had once stood, but once again I was surprised. The place was a time capsule: the great foyer we had entered was at least fifteen feet high and illuminated by a stained glass skylight. Furniture stood nearly intact: divans and wing-back chairs and Tiffany lamps from the turn of the century, all in place, untouched. There were books on the shelves (Moby-Dick, Tess of the d'Urbervilles), a tea service on a pewter platter, and a walking stick still in a stand.

It was as though the occupants and staff had just stepped

out for a breath of air as we'd arrived and would be back any moment.

The Wise Man thumped a pillar with his fist. "No worries about this place coming down around our ears," he said. "Look at these supports." He was right; the walls were held up by doorposts that had to be two feet in diameter. He looked around with admiration. "This was a house built to last."

"But why is it like this?" I asked.

"Why don't you tell me?" He walked over and sat on the second step of a grand staircase that began at the back of the front room and obviously carried visitors to a suite of bedrooms. "What does this place and its condition mean?"

So this would be our classroom. Fair enough. I was game and ready to work my mind after a day of exercising my body. I paced around the lower floor rooms: drawing room, parlor, basic kitchen, office. Everything was that remarkable state of suspended animation. It was quite a mystery. Trying to do my best Sherlock Holmes impression, I surveyed marks in the dust and the placement of the utensils that were still on the table, thumbed a few papers left on the office desk—invoices and correspondence, mostly. The personal stationery gave me the name of the home: Madison Park. Elegant without being pretentious. I liked it.

Finally, I turned back to my companion, who watched me expectantly. "Got a theory?"

I did. "The best I can figure it, whoever lived here was abducted, probably by someone they knew. There is a carving knife and dinner silverware on the dining room table. There's a book on a small side table over by the fireplace; someone was clearly interrupted while reading by firelight. The door was unlocked, and there's no sign of forced entry or any violence at all." I felt like Columbo. "The residents were either kidnapped or arrested in a late-night raid of some kind, probably for being involved in some sort of organized crime."

The Wise Man clapped politely at the end of my speech and stood. "Professor, that was impressive. I noticed that some of the correspondence on the office desk was in regards to legal matters and hidden assets, so I see where you might come to the financial crime conclusion."

"But you don't agree," I said, leaning against the huge door supports, feeling their still-smooth varnished surface under my fingers.

"I'm afraid I don't," he said kindly. "But it doesn't matter that much. I didn't bring you here to play detective."

The Meaning of Meaning

"Well, then where's the leadership lesson in this place?" I asked. "It's wonderful, but I don't really see the point."

He walked into the cluttered private office and waved for me to follow. "Tell me something. Let's say that you're right about what happened here. What does that say about the person who owned this house?"

I put myself into FBI profiler mode. "Well, I'd have to say that on the surface, he was a successful businessman and someone who cared about leaving a legacy, because he built this place to extraordinary standards," I said. "But he also had a hidden life, something illegal that got him and his family arrested or killed. I wonder if somewhere in these hills are some unmarked graves with him, his wife, and his children in them."

I folded my arms, finished with my analysis. The Wise Man nodded, then said, "If this place were a den of immorality and illegality, and you lived in the area, would you feel any guilt about borrowing a few of these beautiful pieces of furniture for your house, or even bringing down a truck to rip up these gorgeous floor planks and transport them back to California to use in a renovation?"

I thought about that one for a while. "I would certainly be more apt to do it if I thought the people who lived here were criminals, yes."

He snapped his fingers. "Exactly! The meaning that you created around this place translated into permissible behavior. That meaning is what this is all about."

I sat down on a musty but otherwise intact ottoman. "All I did was develop a narrative," I said.

He sat opposite me on the floor, Indian-style, where he

seemed to be most comfortable. "Doesn't matter. Meaning and context are behind everything. Every person who encounters or hears about this house assigns meaning to its existence and its vacancy. To you, it was possibly the house of an organized crime lord or Prohibition bootlegger. To that guy at the general store, it's haunted. To someone else, it's a treasure trove of antiques. To another person, it's a commentary on the sorry state of home construction in our age. The point is: left to ourselves, we all decide what things mean based on our experience, prejudices, fears, and passions."

I looked around at the wainscoting, finely carved stair balusters, and stained glass panels and thought that there was meaning contained in every line of this place—the life stories of the craftsmen who built it, the experiences of the various residents, even the histories of the financiers who had made its construction possible. But I didn't see the significance of that meaning beyond its inspiration for storytelling.

"True, but so what?" I said. "I think it's wonderful that such a great old house can inspire so many flights of imagination from so many observers."

"But meaning doesn't stand alone," the Wise Man said gruffly. "That's the point. Meaning permits or provokes action, and if the meaning is based on the wrong interpretation of the information, the action can be destructive or

harmful." He thumped on the wide floorboards with his boot. "If I told you that these boards had come from a dismantled slave ship where thousands of West Africans had died on their way to the cotton fields of the South, that meaning would probably make you feel a hell of a lot better about driving up here some night with a truck and a crowbar, prying a few hundred square feet loose, and taking them to Jackson Hole to become the floor of your new vacation house.

"Meaning is different for every person. That becomes a huge problem in organizations, where the meaning that people assign to events becomes a powerful driver of behavior."

"So the leader," I said after a moment, "is responsible for making sure everyone has the correct story and all the facts so they can attach the right meaning to what happens?"

"No." He stood and walked into a back room that I had not seen yet, a study that reeked of masculinity: mounted animal heads, a great, corroded shotgun on the wall, an old portrait of a gent with muttonchops. My companion walked over to a small table and picked up some papers lying there. "The leader doesn't provide the facts. She creates the meaning. She decides what the official meaning of events is and then hands that down to her followers like Moses handing down the Ten Commandments. Otherwise, everyone chooses his or her own meaning, and you have chaos."

The Benefactor's Departure

That made sense. In a shifting business world and a twenty-four-hour news cycle, context is hard to come by. Yet people still get plenty of information—about layoffs, new inventions, wars, buyouts, and a thousand other things. Without a defined sense of what those things mean for them, they could react in ways that could damage an organization. Some might defect to competitors, steal secrets, panic and become depressed, or take illegal action.

"I see what you're saying," I said. "Meaning is inherent in everything, and a leader has to control it and turn it into an asset. But that doesn't explain this house."

"Of course it does. Professor, have you asked yourself why Madison Park hasn't been looted for all its artifacts?"

I hadn't figured that one out yet.

"It's not because it's supposedly haunted," the Wise Man said. His bright gaze drew me over to stand by the window, where he held up papers so I could read them. I took a look at a florid signature: Frederick K. Madison.

"I've been here before," he said. "The owner and builder of this house was a railroad baron who fell in love with this region and settled here in the 1880s. He immediately became a generous benefactor to the town and the surrounding area. These hills were dirt-poor, and Madison, who came from poor origins, began spending his fortune and building hospitals, schools, churches, an aid society,

*and even one of the first veterinary clinics in the country
for large animals.*

*"Over the years," he went on, "he became a saint to
the people of these villages and hamlets. They loved and
respected him and his family to the point where he couldn't
spend a dime on anything—the farmers would give him
fresh produce and milk, the ranchers would bring over just-
butchered meat, the town doctor wouldn't accept a penny
for a house call, and so on. But it couldn't last. Madison
had spent every penny he had and borrowed more trying to
help these people, and one day the bank came calling."*

*He waved his arm as if to take in the entire expanse
of the great house. "One night, a friend warned Madison
that the next day, foreclosure officers would come and
kick him and his wife and daughters out of their home.
Wanting to spare them the humiliation, he sent them
immediately to their New York townhouse, where two
years later, he took his own life." He looked back at me.
"Ten years after that, a local newspaperman wrote a
feature that told the entire story. So for three generations,
the people of this area have protected the property and
legacy of the man they came to see as their benefactor.
They patrol this house and grounds regularly to make sure
there's no vandalism and keep strangers away. That young
character at the general store was probably a newcomer to
town who didn't know any better."*

I looked down at the letters in his hands. Reading further, I saw that they were warnings from a bank in Connecticut and pleadings from friends to sell Madison Park and return to the city. I had been terribly wrong in the meaning I had found in this house, but it was an instructive lesson in the power of that meaning. "So because thousands of people share the meaning of Madison Park as the legacy of a great man, they've chosen to protect it and keep it intact all these years," I summarized.

The Wise Man set the papers down on the table where he found them.

"Precisely," he said, making his way into the front room. "Imagine the fate of this place if its meaning had been that this was the house of a criminal mastermind. " He shook his head. "That's why an effective leader defines meaning for the led. That's what that newspaperman did."

"When you define meaning and determine the story, you can direct the outcome," I said.

"Yes," he replied. "That's been true from the Nazis to the BP oil spill. It will always be true." He looked back at the perfectly preserved house, a museum of an earlier era. "I still think it would be cool if this place were haunted, though," he said.

I walked past him down the steps. The sun was declining toward the horizon. "Come on," I said. "You said the community polices this place. We don't want to get shot as looters."

He slid his arms through his backpack straps. "That, Professor, is the best advice I've heard all day." Without a word, he retraced his steps across the overgrown field and we made our way back to the fork in the trail, where we would begin to descend down into the wooded valley.

My Thoughts on The Tale of the Empty House

In this chapter, I'll present my views on judgment and meaning, and their impact on a leader's ability to inspire, align and create a narrative story to build followership. I'll also talk about the vital roles that self-honesty and honesty with others play in combating cynicism.

The Tale of the Empty House tells us two important things:

1. We greatly determine how we respond to the events of our lives by the kind of meaning we attach to them.

2. As leaders, if we want to shape the meaning that the people in our organizations ascribe to events, we must first be aware of the meaning *we* attribute to those events.

Remember the parable about the five blind men each feeling a different part of an elephant? Each insists it's a different thing based on the body part he's touching: the guy touching the trunk says the creature is a snake, while the chap with his arms around one of the pachyderm's thick legs insists it's a tree. None of them has enough information to put together the big picture of reality on his own.

In most organizations, from the office to the athletic arena, the individuals in your authority are like those blind men groping for a picture of reality. As the leader, you may be the only one in your organization with eyesight (or better, vision) keen enough to

ISDOM LEADING CONCEPTS

- The leader is the definer of reality and the purveyor of hope

- Defining meaning prevents "mob reality"

- Delusion, a false or distorted belief about self, defies reality and purveys hype

- It is foolhardy to promote or adhere to a personal brand that doesn't reflect reality

- Cynicism is a rampant and corrosive "story" encouraged by false promises

- Epistemic closure locks an organization into a loop of failure

ISDOM LEADING GOALS

- Understanding the leader's role in creating meaning and hope

- Developing tools to prevent uncontrolled meaning from damaging an organization

- Avoiding the blindness to the hard facts that can turn hope to hype

- Becoming aware of your brand, taking control of it, and living up to it

- Preventing the corrosive effects of rampant cynicism

- Learning how to keep your organization from falling into epistemic closure

- Understanding the need to bypass rules and preconceptions to make progress

perceive that the creature in question is, in fact, an elephant. Your board of directors may have a picture that is mostly complete, but because they are not in the trenches every day as you are, they lack your perspective. Even more complicated, others sometimes don't realize that they don't see the whole picture. As a result, they act on incomplete information.

Preventing "Mob Reality" From Taking Hold

The leader has the responsibility to relieve followers from the need to construct their own meaning of the events that affect the organization, team, or family. Left to our own devices, we all form a picture of reality and its meaning—based on whatever incomplete piece of the total puzzle we possess and on our beliefs and fears—conscious or otherwise. Some will look at the empty Victorian house in the field and imagine bankruptcy and foreclosure; others will concoct a macabre story of murder and late-night burials.

It's not hard to imagine how such "mob reality" can wreak havoc on a company. Imagine your company (I call it YourCo) facing a difficult economy and shrinking market share. A news item breaks: YourCo's two main competitors are reducing headcount and handing out layoff notices. The whispers begin: *What does this mean? Are we next? Is my job on the chopping block?* Fear grows. Morale suffers. People mope or resign. If the YourCo leaders don't redefine reality and repair the damage, the company will take a serious productivity hit, forcing it to institute layoffs even if it actually had no plans to do so before the rumors began.

Imagine a baseball team on a five-game losing streak, whose infield has just committed errors on three consecutive plays. If the manager says nothing and lets the team determine the meaning of these events, the players may start to doubt or question the team's true talents, and resignation will likely ensue. They "get back on their heels."

On the other hand, the manager could frame the current reality by reminding the players that every team hits a run of bad luck during a season; obviously, this is theirs. The next inning is a new opportunity to change that. The team takes the field energized and hopeful.

Effective leaders act as filters for outside events and provide people with an honest and productive framework of meaning with which to view them—to see that yes, the individual parts do add up to something recognizable. Rather than allow ad hoc interpretations of things like currency fluctuations, a fall on a balance beam dismount, or an error by the shortstop, leaders should take preemptive action to provide people with an *approved*—for lack of a better word—version of reality before the rumor mill starts to churn.

Defining Reality and Purveying Hope

Later in this chapter you'll meet Deloitte's Maritza Montiel, a longtime coaching client and friend. She taught me that one of the chief duties of a leader is to function as the *definer of reality* and the *purveyor of hope*. Here's what that means:

1. *Defining reality*—People are attending a social gathering at a restaurant and a car speeds by outside, tires squealing. Instantly, everyone in the group, based on individual experiences and biases, forms a narrative to explain the meaning behind the sound. One is certain that the sound means a high-speed police chase is going on. Another hears high school kids drag racing. Yet another will be listening for the inevitable crash of front end meeting tree or lamppost.

No organization can afford so many versions of reality. Since the leader typically has access to most or all of the available information—financials, sales data, team scouting reports—it's his or her responsibility to assemble the *official, non-negotiable* interpretation of reality that will be most beneficial to the organization and then communicate that interpretation to everyone else clearly but without glossing over potentially unpleasant truths. The wise leader of

YourCo might send out an e-mail that reads, "Our competitors are laying people off, and we have it on good authority that they are doing so to be more attractive to a buyer. We see this an opportunity to capture market share and have no plans to reduce headcount in the foreseeable future."

2. *Purveying Hope*—Leaders manage a delicate balance here: cultivating transparency while maintaining security. On one hand, it's important to share pertinent information with your people, even if it's not all rosy. This conveys the respect critical to earning followers' trust. At the same time, it's your role to create a picture of reality that provides hope (if there is cause for any), prevents panic, and keeps people feeling calm, productive and focused on delivering break-through performance. The "No B.S." rule definitely applies here.

Paul Viviano of Alliance HealthCare Services (whom you previously met in chapter one), faced such a dilemma a few years ago after its primary original equipment manufacturer, General Electric, flooded the market with inexpensive diagnostic medical imaging equipment (such as MRI scanners), undercutting Alliance's price point and severely eroding its market share. In the midst of dramatic shifts in the industry and markets and a growing sense of desperation, Paul addressed the firm's leaders and said, "Let me tell you what the industry analysts are saying about us. We have the best management team in the industry, and we fully expect Alliance to survive and thrive and be the industry consolidator in a few years." He also shared important financial data that the managers did not have access to: Alliance's profit margins were north of 30 percent, while its closest competitor's were around 16 percent.

Paul acknowledged the harsh reality but immediately re-framed it and gave it new meaning by reminding people how healthy the company still was. In doing so, he helped those leaders and the company avoid panic and anxiety. He calmed the storm.

Reality without hope is abuse. I have met leaders who were proud of their policy of "keeping it real" but who didn't understand that all they were doing was bolstering their own tough-guy self-image: *Yeah, bring on the bad news. I can take it.* Or coaches whose ego-driven tirades include statements about how badly their team sucks. I've found it serves no purpose to get up in front of a thousand employees at a company retreat and say, "It's likely we're going to have to lay about 20 percent of you off next quarter." I don't care how true that statement is. I don't care if you follow it up with filet mignon and an open bar; you've just shattered your company, team, or family. "Keeping it real" by emphasizing the negative or by ripping your people is not leading. It's terrorizing.

A leader respects his or her people enough to level with them about reality while lending a meaning to reality that gives perspective, allows for hope and suggests a path forward.

LEADERSH*T

Allowing a dozen different realities
to poison an organization,
or sharing the "brutal facts"
without also finding hope within them.

LEADING

Defining reality before anyone else can and in a way
that maintains hope, bolsters morale, and empowers people.

Defying Reality and Purveying Hype?

In my own mind, I'm a loving and attentive father with three kids—daughter Erin is a 28-year-old Northwestern grad, son Lane is a US Army Airborne Ranger sergeant stationed in Italy, and younger daughter Maddi is 18 and is a college freshman at my alma mater, UCLA. In reality, my children have grown up without me around much of the time. Part of building my consulting practice has involved extensive travel, so I was on the road probably 70 percent of the time when my kids were growing up. I know that doing this has enabled me to provide them with a nice standard of living and give them a great education, but "absentee dad" doesn't exactly have the ring of "Father of the Year." So unconsciously, I have maintained a semi-fictional story in my mind.

If I'm committed to be an involved, active father going forward, I have to be aware of the story I'm telling myself *about* myself. It's the stories we tell ourselves about ourselves that govern our experience of life and openness to it. I accept the truth about my parenting choices to date not so I can do penance but so that I can have the perspective to make enlightened choices going forward.

What's your internal story, and what kind of character are you in it? How much of it is true and how much is based on unjustified hope? How much is based on what you *intend* to do but rarely follow through in doing? If your self-image has little connection to reality, you hamper your ability to perceive when you're failing to live up to your responsibilities. You harm others. If you're a leader, instead of being a purveyor of *hope*, you become a purveyor of *hype*.

Great leading means being able to drop pretense and self-delusion, standing naked before ourselves and everyone, and seeing whether the stories that run on our inner movie screens match up to our actions. I've spoken about "performance moments"; it's in those moments that we either live up to our self-crafted story or show it to be pretense.

Here's an example: I accompanied a client's top executives on a team-building trip, river rafting in the Pacific Northwest. It was a marvelous trip filled with wonderful, revealing moments, but one episode perfectly illustrated what I'm talking about.

One C-suite executive, skilled in many things, was completely terrified of the water, to the point where he was angry at me and did not even want to get into a boat.

One of the division presidents put his arm around the man's shoulders and said, "Don't worry; I've got your back."

It was touching and beautiful—until the division president got into another boat! According to this guy's personal narrative, he was the kind of guy who took care of his people no matter what, but his need for adventure seemed to interfere with his self-perception that he was a fierce defender of his friends. If his internal story had been genuine, he would have gotten into the same boat as his terrified colleague and never left his side until they were back on terra firma.

Funny thing: that's exactly what the company's CEO did. He got into the same boat as the water-phobic gentleman, without a word, and stayed by his side for two days. No fanfare, no propaganda. There was symmetry between the CEO's inner story—someone who was concerned about and committed to others' well-being—and his actions. In doing that, he showed why he was a powerful leader.

LEADERSH*T

Maintaining a personal mythology that has nothing to do
with your actions, your decisions, or how you treat people.

LEADING

Admitting that you are just as flawed as anyone else,
but rising above this to establish and keep
a strong, positive brand promise.

As leaders, we should constantly be examining our inner narratives for honesty and currency. Too often we wait for a crisis, such as when someone calls us on an out-of-character decision. But great leaders don't wait. In *Good to Great,* Jim Collins talks about the "mirror/window" philosophy: When things go well, great leaders look out the window to find the other people responsible, and when things go badly, they look in the mirror to discover what they could do better. They also keep people around them who tell it like it is. They value the truth more than empty, comforting pretense.

Why Cynicism Is Like the Creature's Blood in Alien

If you're leading an organization, you're the official source of information, context, and perspective. Whether your people see you as credible has everything to do with how well you have earned their trust by acting in accordance with your intentions and who you say you are. If you lead authentically, trust is strong. You'll be effective at creating meaning and defining reality. If you contradict your story at every step, trust gives way to cynicism.

Remember the movie *Alien?* The alien's blood was an incredibly powerful acid that ate through decks of a space freighter. Cynicism is just as corrosive. If it becomes the most important filter that the people in your organization use to "connect the dots" and create meaning out of what you say, then you're in big trouble.

Cynicism collects around broken promises. The more leaders set expectations and then fail to meet them, the more the confidence of the rank-and-file is shaken. Eventually, the prevailing assumption is that all change programs are hot air, all stories are lies, and nobody has anybody's back. Cynicism is a huge boulder in the stream of any leader making an honest attempt to institute a new order. Think about how your actions contribute to follower cynicism.

In 2002, Hewlett-Packard purchased computer maker Compaq in what was predicted to be one of the most ill-advised mergers in history. The doomsayers proved to be right. HP had been built by founders Bill Hewlett and Dave Packard around "the HP Way" of respect for people and investment in research and development. Unfortunately, in embracing the merger and participating in unprecedented layoffs, CEO Carly Fiorina (perhaps for good reasons) violated that implied promise. The merged company suffered and Fiorina was dismissed. Think about how often this occurs in corporate America.

A counterexample is Dreyer's Grand Ice Cream. In the late 1980s, employees accused leaders of hypocrisy and insisted that they were not practicing the employee-centered values that they preached. Rather than play defense, management took aggressive steps to better adhere to those values and communicate with employees about how they were doing so. Then in 1998, Dreyer's faced a price war while its CEO was battling a brain tumor. The company announced a financial restructuring, and the next day, senior executives fanned out across the country, meeting with every employee to explain what was happening. The employees united in support of the company. Four years later, in a very positive move for the company and its employees, it was acquired by Nestlé.

Failing Before You Try

The effects of cynicism are obvious: despair, ennui, a sense of powerlessness to change anything, minimal effort out of the belief that individual contributions don't matter—and the presumption that nothing works, all promises are empty air, and nothing will ever change.

If I were to design a logo for cynicism, I would make it a pair of rolling eyes. Cynicism breeds the "yeah, right" skepticism that insists that no matter how good the latest five-year plan sounds or how rosy the new team-building initiative seems, nothing will work out as planned.

Leaders train their followers to be cynics when they start things but don't finish them, change directions for no good reason, or launch initiatives that vanish as soon as the wind changes. As the Dreyer's example shows, transparency, proactive communication, and backing up professed values with real action—matching your lips and your feet—is the antidote to cynicism, even in the worst of times.

A Shot of Cuban Spice

I'll give you a great example of how an aggressive insertion of meaning and purpose shattered cynicism. Maritza Montiel is a vibrant, brilliant, fiery woman of Cuban descent who is a senior partner and key leader at Deloitte, the largest privately-held professional services firm in the world. A few years back, she was named Regional Managing Partner of the Central Atlantic region, at the time the worst-performing region in the company. Who knows why she got the promotion, as she had not previously held a position at that level of leadership responsibility. The fact was, she was a Hispanic woman around age fifty and was possibly expected to fail. Instead, she defied all expectations.

The region was infected with rampant cynicism. The default belief at all levels was that nothing would ever change. Upon taking over, Maritza's first act was to redefine reality. She got her team together and told them that within two years, this would be the fastest-growing region in the company.

"The first thing I needed to do was build the trust of my followers," she says. "Without trust, there is very little you can do in leading. The internal mantra was, 'No one really cares about us. They just want to make a lot of money, so they work us to death.'"

She continues: "Six months later, I said, 'You are where you are because you choose to be. If you want a different outcome, if you want to be respected, if you want dominate in the marketplace, you have to take the first step forward. It's not up to the firm, but us.' With every step, it was vital for them to believe we could win."

After even minor account wins, Maritza would make sure that everyone toasted them with champagne. "They were not accustomed to feeling good about themselves," she says. "They were not accustomed to confidence. We shifted the paradigm of the firm to empowerment and belief that we can choose to get out from where we were into something better." Within two years, hers was the fastest growing region in the company, and Maritza was its fastest-rising star.

Never shy about expressing her opinions, she thinks most leaders focus too much on vague things like vision and dreams without preparing people for what it's going to take to make them real. "Leaders think that if they go around and make speeches, good things will happen," she says. "But you can oversell the dream, and unless you have tangible things people can latch onto so they can see the finish line, they think there will be a quick fix. Anyone can come up with a dream or a vision. What's lacking is the specifics: How do we get from here to there? If you're a terrible football team like the Detroit Lions, you don't think about winning the Super Bowl. You think about how to get a lot of little things to go right so you can get from where you are to winning. If you can't convey that, it's hard to get to the goal."

She goes on: "I take the impossible and say, 'What do we have to do the next six months?' If I said, 'We're going to dominate the marketplace in six months,' no one is going to believe me. It's hard to get followership if people can't see the vision laid out, step by step. So you have a relentless focus on the steps, and then when you get a win and people can see the results, they will be on board." To this day, Maritza remains one of the most effective leaders with whom I've had the pleasure of working.

In his landmark book *Man's Search for Meaning,* Victor Frankl writes that meaning leads to purpose, and purpose keeps people alive. In organizations where cynicism and despair are constant risks, the affirmative act of creating meaning around their work helps people keep their heads above water and breathe. It can be as simple as the difference between saying "Nice work last month" and telling a group, "We're the third-fastest-growing division in the company."

LEADERSH*T

Allowing broken promises and lack of accountability to breed cynicism, which undercuts trust and faith in leadership and leader-defined meaning.

LEADING

Backing up intentions with actions and following through on plans, communicating with people clearly at all times, and making it possible for employees to rise to a challenge.

Beware the Closed Loop

Break this one out for your next game of Scrabble: *epistemology.* Epistemology basically means "how we know what we know." It's the study of how knowledge is acquired. If that sounds a little esoteric, bear with me. It's actually quite relevant.

As a leader, your efforts to define reality, create meaning, give hope, and foster trust have a serious purpose: preventing *epistemic closure.* Epistemic closure occurs when any group, company, or team creates its own locked-down information ecosystem where the only knowledge that can get in is that which agrees with and reinforces existing beliefs.

For example, in today's political environment, if you're a conservative Tea Party enthusiast, it's possible for you to immerse yourself in a media world of Fox News, Rush Limbaugh, NewsMax, books by Sarah Palin, and so on. There is no need for you to ever come into contact with any source of information that contradicts your closely held political beliefs. You've created epistemic closure around yourself. The same is true on the other side of the political aisle.

When the official internal culture of a company says that it can do no wrong (or do no right!), any external realities that conflict with that story are likely to be ignored, putting the company in grave danger of disregarding serious threats until it's too late.

This was what happened to the Big Three U.S. automakers in the 1980s. General Motors, in particular, was secure in the self-knowledge that it had always been the world's biggest car company; surely it would continue to thrive—because it was General Motors!

Trapped in its epistemic bubble, the company kept churning out unreliable gas guzzlers while consumers demanded well-made, fuel-efficient cars like the ones from companies like Honda and Toyota. Only recently has GM made a comeback after a three-decade slide and a government bailout; Chrysler has just now begun to breathe new life into its business.

This Is Your Brain on Hope

You have probably seen this brainteaser: nine dots on a page, arranged in a square. The challenge is to connect all the dots without lifting your pencil from the paper. People have a great deal of trouble doing this because they assume that they cannot draw lines that leave the invisible borders of the square, even though *there is nothing in the rules that says so*. In fact, you cannot solve the puzzle unless you go outside the borders.

Most people in organizations, from the regional offices to the C-suite, allow their thinking to be limited by preconceptions and presumed rules. Our minds are brilliant at staying within structures and patterns based on past experience. People in organizations see things happen and their mental algorithms do the calculations: *what happened in the past will happen in the future, in the same way*. Because of this, many people never even consider new ways of doing business, even when the old ways are manifestly broken.

A leader trying to establish a new order of things (to paraphrase Machiavelli) must rewrite those algorithms to allow people to perceive new realities and find new meaning. In a beautiful example, the leaders of the PinnacleHealth System in Harrisburg, Pennsylvania, prepared its managers to implement a significant post-merger culture change by using examples, stories, and videos that highlighted "the old way and the new way"—called it out, drew attention to it, had fun with it. And, in so doing, provided concrete examples of the types of behavior that would be encouraged and rewarded in the new culture.

Banishing cynicism and instituting a culture where management defines meaning and provides hope does not happen overnight. Ask any employee in a place where change was done *to* them. Ask any human being who's been on the receiving end of false promises. Trust grows only where stated values and intentions are backed up by meaningful action, accountability, and transparency. But with patience and attention to the need for hope—as well as respect for the intelligence and passion of employees at all levels—it is possible to turn the ship. I have seen it happen many times, even when wrecking on the rocks seemed inevitable.

ACCESS POINTS

The Tale of the Empty House

Questions I've asked myself and others in our journeys to greater free-dom from judgments, disempowering stories, and epistemic closure:

In what areas of my life are my opinions most fixed or rigid (e.g., beliefs about self, worldview, morality, politics)?

_____

_____

_____

_____

_____

How judgmental am I about others' behavior? In what ways does that serve me? What would become possible if I approached it differently?

_____

_____

_____

_____

_____

When I judge others, what truth about myself is it covering?

_____

_____

_____

_____

_____

When I am upset, how able am I to distinguish between the facts of the situation and the judgment or "stories" I create?

_____

_____

_____

_____

What are the underlying, persistent themes to the "stories" that I keep creating?

_____

_____

_____

_____

What am I serving by keeping those stories (e.g., I'm not good enough, that person is bad/wrong) alive? What's becomes possible if I'm willing to change those stories?

_____

_____

_____

_____

_____

For any event or instance of progress, how well do I satisfy my teammates' "need to know" (rather than what I feel like communicating)? What does having good data and a good frame for understanding it make possible in their performance?

_____

_____

_____

_____

_____

Whose opinion can I seek that will challenge or confront my own?
Who's the "truth teller" in my life?

_____

_____

_____

_____

_____

A Final Thought

One of the most liberating acts in my life has been my work
to find freedom from my own thinking.

FOUR

The Tale of the Storm

Noise is the most impertinent of all forms of interruption.
It is not only an interruption, but is also a disruption of thought.
—Arthur Schopenhauer

After putting our "haunted" house six miles behind us, we were too far from a town to find accommodation, so we camped under the stars. The next morning, as we drank our coffee and prepared for the day's walking, the sky was darkening. To the west, deep slate blue clouds were massing into a squall line. With the mild temperatures we'd been having, I knew that the collision of warm air with the cold mass of the coming storm would likely produce a thunder and lightning show.

The Wise Man had followed my eyes and read my mind. "Yeah, we won't want to be exposed on high ground today," he said. "I think we should go overland and head for that line of trees." He pointed northeast, and I was barely able to make out an expanse of woods about five miles off. "I know there are some shelters we can use if things get nasty."

We downed our java, buried the campfire, and set off for another long day of walking. After about an hour, we veered off the trail and began going overland, which would have been difficult in hillier terrain but was fairly easy on these gradual, gently sloping whalebacks. I kept my eyes on the western horizon, and I could see my companion doing the same. Ramparts of blue-black clouds were piling up like pillows, gorgeous against the tawny golds and browns of the summer grass and fallow farmer's fields. But we could both feel the cold wind blowing ahead of the storm and knew that we had maybe two hours before we started to get wet.

Motivated by a desire for comfort (and not to be caught out in the open if the storm got really violent), we picked up the pace. Shoulder to shoulder, we passed a bag of trail mix back and forth and silently shared the view. That had become our modus operandi: minimal speaking while on the trail, which I loved. I was enjoying the quiet in my own head and the opportunity to take in what I saw without the narrative of anyone else, even someone as learned and interesting as my guide.

The Sky Falls

We almost made it.

About three hours into our hike, I felt the first raindrops hit my face. Looking up, I saw a quilt of restless clouds hanging low over us like a hand ready to swat us down.

110

It was oppressive and beautiful, but I was less impressed when the dime-sized drops started pummeling us.

"Now what?" I said. My companion waved me on and starting walking even faster. "It'll be drier under the trees!" He was correct; we moved deeper among the pines, birches and cedars, and the canopy protected us from the worst of the rain. But we both knew it was going to fall a lot harder, so we were both keen on finding shelter.

As we walked, I noticed the noise: The patter and whisper of rain falling on leaves and needles, the soft finger snap of the stray drop that penetrated the canopy to reach the forest floor. It was mesmerizing and sleep inducing. I felt the urge to curl up with a great book, a glass of wine and some jazz. I thought that it was amazing what noise could do to the thought process. But this was only the beginning of that lesson.

We located a narrow trail along the leaf-strewn forest floor; as we stepped onto it, the skies really opened up. The few drops that found their way to us became multitudes, and within a minute we were soaked. The relaxing sound of moments before had become a freight train bellow. It was deafening. "What now?" I shouted.

My companion, as always, was unflappable. "I'm pretty sure there's a shelter up ahead about a hundred yards," he yelled back. Pretty sure? I was starting to think about rounding up animals two by two. But he quickened his

*pace and dashed up the trail into a thick stand of white
pines surrounded by boulders. I followed, and then we
both saw it at the same time: a small wooden hut, overgrown with moss and practically invisible from the trail
but vivid as the heavy rain splashed on its tarpaper roof.
It looked like a bus shelter; I hoped it was big enough
for two. If not, we were going to have one hell of an arm
wrestling match.*

*"Come on!" He trotted down the other side of the rise
and ducked onto a side trail that led to the shelter. I followed, wondering if we might find ourselves elbow-to-elbow
with other hikers. But when he ducked through the low
entrance (there was no door), the shelter, which was maybe
eight feet square, was deserted. Best of all, it was dry. Whoever had built this little cottage had built it well.*

*The interior was Spartan: two cut logs serving as
benches; a small shelf; and a table with a journal, its pages
curled from the moisture. I quickly leafed through it. The
place felt snug and lived in—and at any rate, we had no
other options. We dropped our packs and sat, listening to
the crash of the rain around us.*

Primordial

*Then came the lightning flashes—not striking near us but
sufficiently bright to flashbulb through the open doorway—
and, after a few seconds, the kaboom of thunder like giant's*

footsteps. Over the tumult, I shouted, "Who built these shelters?" but I couldn't concentrate on the answer. I was becoming unnerved by the noise. Like the sound of a truck unloading a bed of ball bearings, it overwhelmed everything else. Something primal kept warning me that at any moment the roof would collapse, a flash flood would sweep us to our doom, or lightning would strike the shelter and erase us from existence.

The Wise Man was speaking, and over the sounds I could catch occasional words—"back during the Depression," "trail system"—but I was completely thrown. Finally, he saw that I was barely even in the tiny room with him, and he paused in his storytelling.

"Where are you right now, Professor?"

"What?" Another bomb blast of thunder had made me jump. "You're not here. Where are you?"

I blinked and realized that I could hear his voice perfectly well. The rat-tat of the rain and the blast of the thunder were loud, but not that loud. It was as though apprehension had stuffed cotton in my ears, and his question had pulled it out again. Strange. "I don't know," I answered.

He smiled. "The noise got you," he said. "I've seen it happen during these kinds of storms. The noise outside creates noise inside and makes being present impossible."

Boom. Another thunderclap. I forcibly brought myself

back to my present state: seated on a polished log in a small hut, weathering a classic summer thundershower. It wasn't a bad place to be. "I think I smell another lesson in leading," I quipped.

The smile became a grin. "You might at that." He pulled a flask from his pack, took a sip, and offered it to me. "Whiskey, homemade by a guy I know. Good for warming up in this kind of weather." I took it and sniffed the contents. Strong. Sipped it. Smooth and warming. "What did you mean about the noise outside creating noise inside?"

He took back the flask and sipped. "The noise outside triggered a response inside your mind. I could see it. You were fearful, nervous, maybe feeling a little out of control, like primordial forces had you at their mercy. That about right?"

I nodded. I'd felt helpless and diminished.

"Well," he went on, "that inner noise made it impossible for you to be present in the moment and appreciate it. You were everywhere but here: in another location far away from the rain and thunder, in a headspace of confusion over feeling small and fearful and insignificant."

I listened to the sounds around us. They hadn't changed; the rain still hammered furiously on the roof and in the trees, the thunder still cracked, the lightning sometimes struck so nearby that a whiff of ozone hung in the air. But they no longer undercut my ease or made me cower;

now they were just the noises of nature playing out as she always has. I was back in the present.

"You're right," I said. "The noise was like a wind that blew through my mind and pulled me out of the space and time I should have been occupying. It was reflexive. I couldn't help it. Until I became consciously aware of it and willed myself back into the present, I wasn't here with you."

He nodded. "It's not a big leap to see how that could be huge blockage in a leader's stream," he said. "If you're supposed to be present in the moment for your people, yet you let fears, doubts, or worries sweep you away from that moment to another place, you can't lead effectively. I call that noise." He took another sip of the whiskey. "Noise dominates our minds so that we can't see what's really happening around us in the present."

I took the flask back and sipped again. "But now things are different," I said. "The noise is still here; that hasn't changed. But it's no longer sweeping me away. I'm able to tune it out and see it for what it is. That's completely changed my emotions about this situation."

"And now what's your appraisal of it?"

I looked around. The darkness was gone. The fear that some overwhelming force would annihilate us seemed silly. In their place I could feel a growing, almost profound awareness of the significance of what was happening—what it meant in the context of myself and the world.

"I love it," I said. "This is how it's supposed to be. I can see how this weather, this shelter, the people who built it, and the people who live off this land are connected. I feel I can take it all in now and appreciate it."

Leading in the Moment

My companion smiled and slapped me on the leg. "I knew you'd get it. Now, as a leader, if you were letting that flow of constant noise pull you out of yourself and take you somewhere, do you think you could be effective?"

"Of course not," I replied. "A leader who could not inhabit the present moment would have no chance of being there for his people. He would be reacting from regret, paranoia, embarrassment, or some other source of noise, instead of reading the needs of the moment.

"But it doesn't stop with the leader," I went on. I was eager to get this out. "The followers all hear noise even more strongly than their leaders. They worry about losing their jobs, being punished for failures, about work-life imbalance. They are trapped in a downpour of distractions. It's the leader's job to bring them back to the moment as well, and also to build them a shelter from the storm, an environment where noise is minimal."

The Wise Man slapped the wall of the shelter in delight, and as if waiting for his cue, the rain slackened and the noise fell off to a mouse-foot patter. "Beautiful! Yes, a leader leads in the moment; he can't lead in the past or future. If he allows noise to blow his mind out of that moment, he ceases to lead. Leaders manage the noise. It doesn't manage them."

He got up and stuck his head out of the hut. "Oh, come and smell this," he said, and then disappeared. I grabbed my pack and followed. The rain clouds, shattered by the winds, were blowing over like iron filings and leaving dappled sunlight in their wake. Everything smelled freshly washed, renewed.

"Listen," my companion whispered. "Tell me what you hear." I did: dripping water, wind in the pines, the nearby stream flowing with its temporary recharge of water, birds taking to the air again with song, rain-soaked branches creaking.

"Gorgeous, isn't it?" he said. "That's a different kind of noise. We choose to look for it. It's not intrusive. It's subtle, and we can only perceive it when we get rid of the stuff that clogs our minds and suffocates us." He took off his hat, walked over to a huge oak leaf bowed in the middle with a load of water, and tipped the fresh rainwater onto his head. "Oh, that's good."

Without speaking another word, we both headed back for the trail. It was well designed and had drained the water without a hitch. We wouldn't have to walk in mud. We fell back into the cadence of our hike naturally, silently. I wanted to listen, not disrupt the silence. But eventually, I said, "The noise we chose to hear is not really noise at all, is it?"

He slowed so I could catch up. His eyes were sparkling from the experience with the wild weather. "No, it's not. When you shut out the fear, worries about money and your job, and the nagging voices insisting that you're not good enough, you can perceive subtleties that only exist in the moment. In these woods, that means the chuckling of a seasonal stream that will be dry thirty minutes from now. In business, it might be someone's overlooked but brilliant idea, or a few words that can give someone confidence."

"When we pay no attention to the noise, we can really start listening," I said. We were walking the bottom of a long saddle in the trail and I could see that on the other end, we would emerge into lighter trees and then daylight. The sun streamed down as though the storm had been a bad dream.

My guide clapped me on the shoulder. "Professor, there may be hope for you yet. Come on. If we can get to the road, we can hitch a ride into the next town, and I know a fantastic restaurant. Unless," he said with a broad grin, "a night in a warm bed doesn't appeal to you."

I was the first one on the side of the country highway with my thumb out.

My Thoughts on The Tale of the Storm

In this chapter, I will explore the issue of noise, the distractions and psychological detritus that fragment our minds and prevent us from performing in the moment. I'll look closely at the impact of noise on sports performance, examine the concept of innate genius, and ask why business can't be more like hockey and have a penalty box where failures are erased.

In my work with the UCLA softball team, few things were more confounding during the 2010 season than the performance of Kaila Shull. Shull, the Bruins' starting senior catcher, had stopped hitting. Another of the team's star players had gotten in a mental soup, and Kaila, a team leader, had decided she was responsible for helping her teammate out. This monster distraction ejected her from the quiet space inside her own head and made it impossible for her to perform at her best in the moment. At one point in the season, her batting average hovered around an abysmal .150.

Knowing that she was a tough, talented young woman the team was going to need if it was to win an NCAA title, I worked with Kaila to help her keep her stream clear of chatter and negative self-talk arising from the situation with her challenged friend and teammate. By season's end, it had worked: she raised her average to .336 and was named to the All-Pac-10 Honorable Mention team. During the Women's College World Series finals, the noise of the moment and the huge stage threatened to derail her train of success. What did she do? She made a list—in the middle of Game One of the finals. This is one important story the ESPN cameras missed.

After walking back to the dugout following her second consecutive strikeout, rather than giving in to the noise in her mind, Kaila found a piece of paper and began to write down all the things that were inside her head, causing noise that distracted her. The items flowed; the list grew almost by itself. Once done, she tore the list up and threw it away, symbolically discarding the clatter that was

ISDOM LEADING CONCEPTS

- Noise kills poise

- Noise comes in internal and external varieties

- Each of us has an inner terrorist who criticizes and undermines us

- We also possess an inherent genius that we can express if we can get past the noise

- In business, failure tends to follow the people who fail; what's needed is a "penalty box" that would allow us to take risks without fear of stigma

ISDOM LEADING GOALS

- Understanding the power of noise to block performance

- Understanding how eliminating noise enables breakthrough results

- Identifying and blocking the inner terrorist

- Discovering your personal genius and its expression

- Overcoming the desire to make failure personal; rewarding bold failures as long-term assets preventing her from being in the moment. Silly, right? Not for Kaila. At the hands of the same pitcher who had dealt her two previous strikeouts, she had a key double in the seventh inning that scored the tying run, sending the game into extra innings where the Bruins won in the eighth. In the second game, Kaila had a single, a run, and two walks as UCLA clinched the title.

Congratulating that young woman on the ASA Hall of Fame Stadium dirt after the trophy ceremony was one of my proudest moments in all my years as a teacher and guide. She managed something that many corporate leaders three times her age still haven't mastered: *getting out of her own way.*

Poise, Not Noise

Kaila's story is one of poise triumphing over noise. Noise shatters the clear thought process, turns us into poster children for attention deficit disorder, and robs us of our power to lead through delivering in performance moments. Noise can be anything: criticism from your boss, unwelcome expectations, self-judgment, fear, even 10,000 fans screaming insults about your mother. Noise is anything that stands in the way of you being fully present and performing at your peak.

Poise, on the other hand, is about blocking the chatter, fears and "what ifs" so that you can bring your mind to the present and deliver what you're capable of delivering. It's grace under pressure. In sports, it's called being a "clutch" player. When we banish noise from our restless brains, we're all capable of coming through in the clutch.

Internal and External Noise

Noise comes in two types—*external* and *internal.* Every person's world is a microburst of external noise. We carry BlackBerries, iPhones, and iPads so we can send and receive e-mails and text messages from Tahiti to Timbuktu. Ads, Facebook updates, and tweets complete for space in our brains. We become coconspirators in this siege when we agree to be on call at all times. But this isn't just about fear of being fired for failing to pick up a call from the boss at two a.m. on Christmas morning. Our near-phobic terror of a silent, unoccupied mind is really a terror of solitude—of our own reflections. What might we discover if forced to face our raw, unfiltered stream of consciousness?

That leads us to internal noise. It's the sometimes dark and disturbing mental traffic that yammers in the background all day and night, nagging us with worries about things we might have forgotten, whispers that we aren't good enough, regrets over something we said in the last meeting, anxiety over an upcoming date or doctor's appointment, or anger over a perceived slight. Internal noise is a psychological and emotional terrorist always looking for weak spots to exploit.

LEADERSH*T
Letting external and internal noise crowd out our ability to be mindfully present and do the work we're capable of.

LEADING
Clearing away the noise to let our ability and presence come through in critical performance moments.

Any kind of noise is a blockage in your stream. When the CEO of a company needs to talk with a key member of the board of directors about serious problems, in that moment she needs to be courageous and candid. If fear makes her pull her punches, she does the company a disservice. Nobody wins. Noise holds us back from the radical honesty that's necessary to lead.

External noise may be frustrating and splinter your concentration with constant interruptions, but it's internal noise—with its AK-47 rattle of doubts, fears, grudges, pressures, and regrets—that prevents us from showing up fully for those we purport to lead. It's internal noise that I will dwell on for most of this chapter.

Sports and the Mental Game

To many of the executives I coach, it comes as a shock that we actually don't have the power to shut our inner terrorist up—not and still function as leaders, anyway. Don't think so? Try this: *Stop thinking.* Stop the flow of analysis, judgment, memory and anticipation that's part of consciousness. Try it now. I'll wait.

Not easy, is it? Your mind was built to think. Remember the exercise where my colleague had the executives sit in silence, and how hard it was for them? That's because the mind craves expression. Only in deep meditation—and with substantial training—can we turn off our cognitive processes and just take in stimuli. I don't think I'll get there in my lifetime!

Our terrorist is always planting bombs that say we don't have what it takes, we're going to blow it, or the people who claim to support us are really plotting against us. However, *we don't have to listen.* You can notice that inner voice spouting its venom, see it for the garbage it is, and tune it out. That's presence. That's choice. That's power. Executives and other leaders who show up powerfully and deliver in critical performance moments don't have some superhuman ability to shut down the self-sabotaging voices. They recognize the lies and ignore them.

Aroldis Chapman, a left-handed pitcher for the Cincinnati Reds, has an incredible fastball that's been clocked at 105 miles per hour. At that speed, if you're standing at the plate with a bat in your hand, you have 0.3 seconds to react and swing at a pitch. If there's the slightest noise in your head—fear, doubt, anger over the ground ball you kicked—you're out. Yet some hitters manage to connect with this fireball. They have clear streams; they are shutting out the noise. The only difference between warning-track power and a home run is confidence that you have what it takes to hit the ball out. That takes a very quiet mind.

Some athletes know that their opponents are poor at shutting out doubt and fear, so they play the mental game like virtuosos. Australian triathlete Chris "Macca" McCormack, the 2010 Ironman World Champion, is famous for his crushing psychological strategy. In his book *I'm Here to Win,* he describes his process of creating mental "folders" in his mind and the minds of opponents like the folders on a computer desktop.

When facing the excruciating pain of a triathlon, McCormack writes, there will come a time when the mind says to the body, "You can't take any more of this! Stop!" His strategy is to have folders in his head—pre-loaded with positive self-talk, confirmation of his training, or reminders of how he overcame the same challenge in a past race— that he can access instantly when the pain comes. Knowing that he can't shut down the noise, he controls it and gains power from it.

At the same time, he also openly talks about the weaknesses of his top opponents, working on their psyches to plant doubt-filled noise in their minds, so that when faced with the choice between agony and perseverance, they give themselves rationales to quit. He writes,

> If they're side by side with me in a race, I want the folder in their head to open and them to think, "Man, Macca's in control. I don't think I can go head-to-head with him." Even sweeter: "Macca called it. He predicted this!" If they think I know something they don't, that's a huge edge for me.

By the time the Women's College World Series 2010 rolled around, the women on the UCLA Softball team were very good at shutting out noise and cultivating poise. They came to the field without noise cluttering up their minds and laid a beating on the other team. Banishing the noise gave them access to their genius.

LEADERSH*T

Allowing deliberate or inadvertent actions
to plant disruptive noise
in our heads or the heads of others.

LEADING

Clearing away the noise to let our ability and presence
come through in critical performance moments.

There's a Genius Inside You . . . and Me

Everyone has a distinctive set of talents, tools and capabilities that are unlike those of anyone else. When you clear away the noise, get out of your own way, and fully express those talents, tools, and capabilities in the moment, you are acting with genius. That potential is always present in you. It's present in everyone working under you.

The noise might be pretense about who you are, fears that you don't really belong, past failures, or anything else that distracts and preoccupies you. The straightest path between here and breakthrough leading is subtraction—getting out of the way of the natural expression of your own greatness. Genius is like one of those secret tracks that some bands put on their music CDs—always there, but hidden until you tune out everything else and seek them out. Once you find them, magic happens.

Turning the noise into poise became a major theme in my work with the 2010 UCLA gymnastics team. Early in the season, the team struggled on the balance beam. If you have to do a backflip on a four-inch-wide piece of wood and your mind is doing anything but focus on the present, you're going to fall. That's what was happening. After the athletes, the coaches, and I worked together to introduce and practice addressing noise and clearing their streams, they found their genius. Their performances on the beam soared.

When our stories are not fully empowering, they become noise. They take us either into past grief over what can't be changed or future worry over what might happen. When we find a clear, calm center, we are able to stop reacting to external events and shut out the noise.

LEADERSH*T

Suppressing your genius or that of your people by allowing pressure, unregulated emotion, or negative self-talk to block natural strengths.

LEADING

Stripping away distractions and blockages
to allow at-will access
to the flow of unique genius
already present in everyone.

Why Business Should Be More Like Hockey

Because you are in a position to lead, solving the problem of noise is not just about your own performance, but also that of all those following you. It is your job to develop a focus of quiet confidence that helps your employees perceive their own inner terrorists and render them powerless by tuning them out.

Typically, this essential leadership function takes two forms. It comes first when you find that place of calm and presence in yourself and carry it with you for all to see. That's leading by example. It comes next when you create an environment in which internal and external noise diminish or vanish, encouraging the led to see their own calm and courage.

The importance of environment cannot be overstated. Sometimes, performance has nothing to do with your ability and everything to do with the conditions under which you perform. Three hundred actors might audition for a role, but the fact that only one will be cast doesn't mean the other 299 are incompetent. Mark Victor Hansen and Jack Canfield sent their idea for the book *Chicken Soup for the Soul* to 130 publishers before one finally bought it and spawned a global bestselling franchise. It's not that the book was bad; the conditions just weren't right.

In business, reducing noise often comes down to creating an environment where the occasional failure is tolerated and even encouraged. This is why I say that business should be more like hockey. In hockey, there's a penalty box. When you deliver a bone-rattling hit on an opponent and the official judges it to be unfair, you spend a few minutes in the penalty box. When your time is up, you go back on the ice and play as if nothing happened. No badge of failure, no scarlet letter. The penalty box is a confessional where you receive absolution for knocking some poor guy's fillings into the fourth row. While you're there, you have a brief respite to gather your thoughts and return to the moment.

Despite what they say, few businesses operate in this way. Few organizations do an adequate job distinguishing between the act of taking a worthwhile risk that doesn't work out and the person who took the risk. This unfortunate ethos has two consequences:

1. It discourages many individuals at all levels from proposing or enacting ideas that come with serious risk, even when the potential upside is a tremendous benefit to the organization.

2. It breeds a culture of fear-based noise in which people worry that any kind of failure will be detrimental to their careers. The running inner monologue is dominated by phrases like "I can't do that" and "What will happen if it's not perfect?"

Businesses that create ecosystems of fear and loathing embody leadersh*t. I have yet to see one where the leaders were getting breakthrough performance or the employees felt full engagement or loyalty. Like British naval warships of the Napoleonic era, such organizations can function based on the crew's terror of the lash, but they don't function well. They tend to hemorrhage their best people and fall behind competitors who are taking wise risks; if they succeed for a while, they do so through brute force.

In contrast, organizations run by wise, breakthrough leaders separate the risk takers from their risky ventures. They know that when you are playing fully and mindfully in an organization, you are going to make errors. Part of creating a "safe haven" from internal noise is creating a culture that encourages smart, bold risks with big upsides and rewards the initiators *whether those risks pay off or not*. Leading is about appreciating that the *process* of developing individual followers' personal genius matters more than the short-term results they produce from any single effort.

LEADERSH*T

Institutionalized punishment for failure
even when the risk is creative, courageous,
and potentially very beneficial.

LEADING

An atmosphere in which helping people develop
the vision, confidence, and passion to take audacious risks
is more important than whether every risk pays off.

In softball, I don't care if you strike out in your first three at-bats as long as you are fully present and ready to play when you come to the plate the fourth time. If you go one for four but drive in the winning run during your last at-bat, who (other than an overzealous parent) cares what you did in the first three? In a properly led organization, failure doesn't follow people. Its followers don't hear those mental terrorists whispering to them about the dire consequences of failure and undermining their confidence. They feel free and empowered to take risks, create, and grow.

The Anti-Vision

For every noise source setting a tiny terrorist loose in your gray matter, there is at least one remedy that can suppress or quiet the noise. For me, *mindlessness* is a stubborn noise source. When I'm mindless, I'm paying attention to the minutiae of life—for instance, feeling compelled to attend to e-mail when it comes in. Instead of giving in to mindlessness, I strive to make each day that I work mindful, strategic, and purposeful. I measure its success by how much I am advancing my life's mission. I don't always succeed, but that's not the point.

Do you have a vision statement? It's important to define what you want to accomplish. However, if your mind is on the fourth quarter instead of the present moment and its challenges, you're like the wide receiver who catches a sure touchdown pass and starts celebrating a bit too soon, only to trip over his feet and fumble on the way to the end zone. The future is noise. Control the only moment that you can: the present moment. When we start "playing to the scoreboard," we've lost. Vision is a touchstone for why we're doing something, but great results come in performance moments.

Success also creates expectations, and there may be no greater source of noise. As one of a handful of consultants in this field who has worked in both locker rooms and boardrooms, I've had a unique chance to compare how head coaches and C-suite executives cope with pressure and expectations. Let me tell you, they are very much alike: trophies, rings, and prizes can make them stupid and forgetful. Victory is like childbirth; it makes painful memories go away so that you only remember the outcome. Even though I see those memories as rich veins of gold to mine, companies and sports teams don't want to dwell on the painful lessons they learned in the past year. They just want to spray champagne after the big win or the big contract.

But the noise of expectations is deafening. That's what makes the great coaches and managers in sports so exceptional. John Wooden and the UCLA men's basketball team, Phil Jackson and the Los Angeles Lakers, and Joe Torre and the New York Yankees were able to repeat championships *despite* their previous triumphs. Believe me, having a big win in your back pocket is not an asset. That trophy weighs tons. Expectations and questions start to whisper and they don't stop until they're screaming.

When I worked with the UCLA softball squad, I sensed that some players were feeling the enormous weight of a program that had dominated the sport for years and was now struggling to regain that glory. One of the first things I asked them was "How many championships has this team won?"

LEADERSH*T

A brutal, emotionally insensitive and warlike
business culture that teaches people
that the short-term outcome is all that matters.

LEADING

A life-affirming, emotionally intelligent culture
that rejects phony machismo in favor of
personal development and tools that help people
shut out noise and be fully present.

They gave me a number, and I replied, "No. This team has won zero titles. This *program* has won championships, but this team has won nothing." That shook some, while others nodded in understanding. It reminded everyone that they were starting from scratch, like every other team in the country. It was a reboot of their expectations of themselves. The moment you're thinking about repeating what you've done, you're out of the moment and a slave to the noise. If you can let it all go and get out of your own way, marvelous things can happen.

ACCESS POINTS

The Tale of the Empty House

Questions I've asked myself and others in our journeys to greater self-expression and performance through recognizing and quieting our internal noise:

When I'm not playing fully in life, what is the internal dialogue that keeps me playing small?

_____

_____

_____

_____

_____

What type(s) of noise (e.g., expectations of others, external feedback, self-critique/evaluation, the pressure of the moment) most negatively affect me?

_____

_____

_____

_____

_____

What's my role in creating my own noise?

_____

_____

_____

_____

What types of noise do I let affect me personally? Why?

_____

_____

_____

_____

_____

When I'm hearing (and present to) the noise, what are the most effective ways for me to dismiss or disregard it?

_____

_____

_____

_____

_____

When am I willing to risk and take chances (e.g., working toward a vision of something better, letting go of the noise)?

_____

_____

_____

_____

_____

What are some habits or rituals that will help me quiet or prevent my noise?

_____

_____

_____

_____

_____

A Final Thought

I know myself to be talented, passionate, loving, and creative, and when I'm not experiencing my life that way, removing the boulder called noise is my first and best remedy.

FIVE

The Tale of the Old Bull

Wisdom is not a product of schooling
but of the lifelong attempt to acquire it.
—Albert Einstein

e found our way to a small city of a few thousand people tucked into a pass between two lines of moderate hills that would be called mountains in these parts. The walking was becoming easier as I felt myself becoming slightly more fit. The air no longer burned in my lungs after six or seven hours of relentless hiking, and my knees didn't throb. What hadn't improved was the weather: after we located a decent motel and spent a night regaling the neighbors with my famous "Nasal Sonata in D Minor," I woke and saw rain coming down in sheets of gray metal.

Damn. It would be an uneventful day, I presumed. Naturally, I was wrong.

I found the Wise Man sitting in the lobby, drinking coffee and looking sourly out the window at the monsoon that had dropped itself on our doorstep. He nodded when he saw my

expression. "Looks pleasant, don't it?" he said with the jovial-
ity with which one sometimes presents bad news. "This won't
be us huddling in some shelter snug as bugs while the rain
passes over. This storm is supposed to last all day."

"I don't mind walking in the rain," I replied. To my sur-
prise, I found that I didn't. I was getting into the physical
and metaphysical nature of this journey and didn't want to
break the rhythm.

He hooked his thumb at the desk clerk. "Wanting doesn't
have much to do with it, I'm afraid," he said. "I asked the
clerk and he told me that all the trails in this area are
washed out and impassable. So I don't think we're going
anywhere today."

I looked back out at the wall of water punctuated by dis-
tant thunder. If we weren't going anywhere in this weather,
what would we do?

The Pasture

Answer: be bored.

I'm not easily bored. As someone who finds nearly every
aspect of human behavior interesting, I can cook up an
anthropological expedition in a crowded airport terminal
or do clandestine psychological fieldwork by observing the
people in line at the DMV. But that requires people, and
as we wandered the small town (population about 3,000,
we learned from the heavily pierced, tattooed clerk) under

borrowed umbrellas, we found that we were just about the only people around.

There was the local general store, mostly empty. The library, also empty but for two librarians. The bookstore, with one browser and a surly-looking clerk. Maybe it was the rain or the fact that most of the people in town were at work in the nearby furniture factory, but there was not a car on the street except for the postal carrier's truck. He honked and waved to us as if we were locals. I was glad we weren't. What a dead little place, I thought.

Then, salvation. In making our third circuit of the tiny downtown, an apothecary (yes, they still exist) told us about an old hunting lodge about a mile outside of town. Good food, good conversation, lots of interesting locals and out-of-towners. But could we walk a mile in this rainy mess, he asked? For the company of other humans who just might tell a good yarn about the time they killed a ten-point buck with a slingshot, I'd walk ten miles in a hurricane.

The lodge was indeed old fashioned and very inviting: an imposing stone structure with a peaked slate roof and mas-sive columns made of raw-hewn Douglas fir trunks. It looked like heaven and became more so when we stepped inside to find a lively tavern with live music and a collection of colorful folk. We greeted the bartender, grabbed a couple of Irish coffees to beat back the chill of the rain, and took a seat near a broad picture window overlooking a hilly pasture. It was cozy and warming in the way that a setting can only be when it provides safety from inclement weather. We settled in to spend the day here among the living.

After a few minutes, the Wise Man pointed down into the pasture. I looked and saw a collection of at least fifteen cows grazing in spite of the pounding rain. Above them, on the slope, a young bull strutted. From the thin woods at the top of the pasture emerged an older bull, horns worn from years of use and mottled coat flecked with white. He was larger than the young bull and calm, as if he had all the time in the world.

"Reminds me of the old joke about the old bull and the young bull," my companion said. "You know the one?" I did. The young bull boasts about running down the hill and romancing some of the cows at the bottom. The old bull, patient and wise, suggests they walk down and conserve their energy for what matters: seducing all the cows.

"You think that young bull would make a good leader?" he asked, eyes twinkling over the rim of his coffee cup.

I pondered. "No, probably not. He'd be reckless and constantly wasting energy on the wrong thing."

My friend shook his head. "That's close, but it's not the heart of the matter," he said. "Think about it, Professor. In that old bull/young bull joke, what's most important to the young bull?"

"Feeling macho, I guess," I said after a minute's contemplation. A nod. "And the most important thing to the old bull?"

"Getting results. He's judging the situation and making an appropriate decision. The young bull is all about serving his ego."

"Correct." He raised one finger and a waitress came over to the table. "Two more Irish coffees, extra Irish," he said, and she glided away. "The old bull considers. He doesn't react. He knows what his final objective is, and reaching it is more important than looking like a badass. The young bull is a bundle of hormones and reactions." He leaned forward over the table. "Effective leaders use their intellects, not their guts. They slow things down and expand the time between their desires and what they do to fulfill those desires. That's what lets them maintain their cool when everyone else is losing it. Ah, thank you."

The waitress slid two steaming drinks across the table, along with a bowl of pretzels. I hadn't expected to find a lesson in leading in this rain-soaked little burg, but here it was. I knew that he was right: the finest leaders I had worked with all possessed the ability to avoid being bundles of reactive triggers. They didn't do things to assuage their egos or to get some sort of adrenaline rush out of lashing out at a low-level manager. They read their own responses, were present in the situation, and acted based on conscious choice.

I also knew that kind of wisdom doesn't always correlate with age. You can accelerate the development of wisdom by cultivating its best qualities: thoughtfulness, mindfulness, authenticity, and presence. The best leaders I knew all possessed them, regardless of their ages. Being the old bull, it seems, doesn't depend on your years but the learning you pack into them.

"I think that's something that only comes with experience," I finally said. "Generally, yes. You're right. And I'll give you an example."

The Orphaned Calf

"I spent a few years working on a farm in southern Missouri when I was in my twenties," he began, the timbre of his voice mixing pleasantly with the low murmur of the tavern's crowd. "One summer, we had several misfit animals: a donkey, a llama, a pig, and an old bull I named Jack because he reminded me of Jack Palance. These critters didn't really belong anywhere, so the rancher put them all together in a fenced pasture and they got along fine. It was really odd, but it worked.

"So it went until August, when one of the cows died giving birth to her only calf.

Normally, the other cows would take over raising the orphan, but they all took a dislike to the little guy, who we named Buster. We were at a loss. We bottle-fed him, but he needed to socialize. The only option was to put him in with Jack and the other misfits and hope they would adopt him.

"What we didn't know until later was that Jack was actually Buster's father, and when Buster came sniffing around trying to make friends, the old bull saw him as a threat to his dominance. I was out cleaning up one day when Buster got under Jack's skin one too many times. What happened next was really extraordinary. Jack lifted a huge rear hoof and looked for sure like he was about to deliver a kick that would have killed the calf instantly.

"Only he didn't. At the last second, I could see the swing of his leg ease up, and instead of kicking Buster he just gave him a 'steer clear' shove, which still knocked the little guy a good ten feet. But I was amazed. Instead of reacting like an alpha male and striking out, Jack had deliberately held back. He ended up becoming Buster's protector. It was one of the most amazing things I've ever seen."

I chewed on that for a long time. "That was what made Jack the leader of the ranch," I said. "Not his power, but his judgment and restraint."

"Exactly," the Wise Man said, draining his cup. "He kept his eyes on the goal—order and dominance—rather than serving his own temporary irritation." He stood up and gestured at the window. "It's letting up." Sure enough, it was. The clouds were breaking and spots of sun were producing multiple rainbows.

"Want to see what the trail looks like?" I said. "That's the best idea I've heard all day."

Near-Collision

It turned out that it was. About a quarter mile from the lodge, a gravel-covered trail arced away from the town and over a series of rocky hillocks in the northwesterly direction that we wanted to go. Because it was on higher ground and built on a gravel substrate, the path was relatively dry and firm, and we made great time. With the rain past, the clouds parted and the sun came out in a sky dappled with gray and white. It was a gorgeous change to the day, and I took off my jacket as the afternoon promised to become fine and warm.

We veered right and down a hill, turning northward into an area that I could see was crisscrossed with numerous side trails, which made me wonder about the type of traffic we might encounter. For the time being, we had the hills all to ourselves, moving along their crests quickly until we entered the tree line, climbing and then descending along a creek lined with young spruce and pine trees. "This looks like an area that was logged not too many years ago," I called ahead to my companion.

He answered without turning around, so he could watch his footing. "Yes, this entire region was pulped about thirty years back," he said. He stopped and was turning to say something else when I saw his eyes widen. I looked over my shoulder and, to my horror, saw a man on a mountain bike barreling toward me from a side trail I hadn't realized was there.

Without thinking, I threw myself out of the way as the bike careened by, not even slowing. It threw up a cloud of dirt and small rocks, some of which collided painfully with my head. "You idiot!" I shouted at the biker's back as he vanished down the trail, caught in the grip of gravity. I stood up and dusted myself off, cursing under my breath.

The Wise Man was at my side, and I expected him to ask about my well-being. But instead, he said with a slight chuckle, "You know, he was at least four feet from you when he went by. You didn't need to jump out of the way."

I didn't know what to say to that. My heart was pounding, my hands shaking. I had reacted out of fear; what did it matter whether the jerk had really been about to use my ribcage for a bike basket or not? "You're not going to tie this into that whole young bull-old bull thing, are you?"

He grinned, brushed some of the dirt from my pack, and led me down the trail. "Let me ask you this. Why did you react the way you did?"

"I told you, I thought he was going to hit me."

"Okay, but to an objective observer, he wasn't that close to you," he said. "Why weren't you objective?"

"I was afraid of being injured. I didn't have time to

analyze what was going on." He winked as though I'd made an important point. "Exactly. Fear takes over and causes us to react instead of thinking and observing. You were like the young bull who uses his gut instead of his brain. If you hadn't been in the grip of fear, you would have been better able to see his trajectory and stay clear with no trouble. That would have been the old-bull move."

I pondered this as we snaked downhill along a series of wide, lazy switchbacks though the trees. Had I overreacted? It was possible. "If I'd been aware of my triggered reaction, I could have slowed things down and made a better choice," I said. "That's what you're saying."

"Yessir." He drank from his water bottle with relish. "That's what a leader does. Even when someone under his command is acting like an idiot, he doesn't allow himself to be goaded into acting on reflex. He sees all sides of the situation and sees the person involved for what or he she really is, not as his or her behavior in the moment."

He jumped over a ditch in the trail, and I followed. As I did, I slipped on the edge and started to go down. But instead of panicking, I found my mind racing in response to what had just happened. Be present, *it said.* Consider. *I considered, found my footing, and cleared the ditch. Why hadn't I done that with the biker?*

"Nicely done," the Wise Man said. I looked ahead and we were coming into a clearing that looked like a staging area

for hikers and mountain bikers. There was a small ranger station, a message board, a potable water fountain, and several benches and trashcans. "You kept your cool and saw the situation as it was. That's what slowing down the game and being conscious of your own thought process does for you. It opens your eyes to the whole picture—or the whole person. You're not making a decision based on one bit of information gained from one momentary slice of time."

The Mountain Biker

Coming into the clearing, I saw the mountain biker who had nearly (or not so nearly) run me down. Clad in green waterproofs and a bike helmet, he looked bedraggled and shaken. Feeling like a fool, I started to walk over to apologize for being such a drama queen. Before I could take two steps, he rode over to me, got off his bike, and stuck out his hand.

"I am so sorry," he said as I shook the hand. "I was out of control up there and didn't know how to stop. Today was only my second time on a mountain bike, and I think it was more than I bargained for."

"Hey, it's all right," I said. "No harm done." Then I swung around to point a finger at the Wise Man. "You wipe that smug smile off your face. I know exactly what you're thinking." The smile broadened into a grin. He clearly found this situation—my not getting the whole picture of the biker

because I had reacted with such hysteria—to be funny. I had to agree with him.

"Hey, are you guys hiking this range?" the biker said. "Yes." I offered him a bottle of water, which he accepted.

He drank a long pull and then pointed to the northwest. "Well, if you're trying to make it to the next town, go into the woods on that fire road there. Take that for about two miles, and then you'll merge into an old paved road that hasn't seen a car in about fifty years. I use it when I want to make great time, and after all the rain, it's the only trail in this area that won't be quicksand. Try it."

I felt a sinewy hand clap my shoulder. "Thanks, son," the Wise Man said. "That's great advice. I'm glad we almost ran into you—or you almost ran into us."

We shared a laugh at that, and then he excused himself and rode off to his fellow cyclists. Without a word, my companion hoisted his pack and led the way toward the fire road at the base of the staging area. We headed into nice country along a split-rail fence, bordered by dense stands of blackberry bushes. I gathered a few berries; thanks to the rain and summer heat, they were lush and delicious. After a mile or so, true to the cyclist's word, we ran into a cracked and grass-grown but straight road that ran almost true north toward blue mountains. It was a dry, perfect surface, and we stepped up our pace.

"Nice fella," the Wise Man remarked.

"Good thing we got to know who he really was instead of just assuming he was some careless, crazy biker, wasn't it?" I said, tongue firmly in cheek.

My companion looked back, and then did something I didn't understand. He stopped dead, then stood to the side and waved his arm for me to pass. I paused, confused, then it hit me. For the first time, he was asking me to lead. Feeling straighter and fresher than I had in days, I walked past him, set my hand on his shoulder for a fleeting second, then took point position as we made our way along the old country road into the trees.

My Thoughts on The Tale of the Old Bull

In this chapter, I'll talk about the concept of wisdom as a "secret" of great leading. Wisdom is defined here as the ability to control one's emotional reactions and allow principles, reason, and knowledge to prevail in determining one's actions. Great leaders can resist natural impulses to react reflexively and instead consider the person, situation, and consequences before responding rationally and wisely—as the Old Bull does.

Leading well in any field hinges on the personal qualities that form the foundation of who you are. Call that character, knowledge, experience, savvy, what have you—I call it Wisdom Leading. Instead of focusing only on tools that are only as effective as the individual who wields them, this philosophy aims to shape the leader as a whole person—head, hands, heart, and spirit. More on each one later in this chapter, but first, let's return to the idea of the old bull.

ISDOM LEADING CONCEPTS

- The young bull reacts based on ego; the old bull considers and acts based on what will serve his goals

- Leading is first about who you are being, then about what you are doing

- We all carry patterns of survival behavior from early life that can be triggered by certain situations

- These triggers set off our fight-or-flight response and cause the knee-jerk reactions that undermine leading

- Leading effectively means mastering these reactions and expanding the time between stimulus and response

- Essence, not ego, is the heart of great leading

 ISDOM LEADING GOALS

- To develop the ability to "slow the game down" and respond consciously to stimuli instead of simply reacting

- To reveal our essence and set aside ego

- To be fully present and see our emotional triggers being tripped so we can control them

- To recalibrate our sense of reward in order to take pleasure in being wise and doing things right rather than in dominating others and venting rage

- To discover what goals we serve and how we can become the people who will serve those goals

Old Bull Versus Young Bull

If you've ever worked with me in a coaching or consulting capacity, you're probably chuckling right now, because you know how much I love to use the example of the old bull. It's a folksy illustration of a fundamental phenomenon that exists in every human enterprise. The youngster is full of raw ability and firepower. He makes snap judgments and often acts on pure adrenaline. He's like a stud rookie pitcher who thinks he has to throw every pitch at ninety-nine miles an hour to get hitters out.

I've repeatedly witnessed this phenomenon in boardrooms, athletic teams, and families. It's the age-old duality of action versus discernment, energy versus experience. In families, it's the parents who help guide the actions of their kids—blurs of energy without the benefit of experience or judgment—to keep them safe. In business, clichés aside, the Ivy League MBAs are literally the smartest people in the room, with incredible analytical talents. But despite their incredible intellectual firepower, few are effective leaders. They often demonstrate low levels of emotional intelligence and poor judgment of people and situations. They haven't yet learned to appreciate that human beings are not always rational and predictable, and they often care more about showing off their intellects than bringing out the best in others. Classic young bull behavior.

In contrast, the old bull cares little about impressing anyone, but he cares deeply about getting results. He's like the old pitcher with the rubber arm who changes speeds, throws junk on the corners, and drives batters crazy—but still gets outs and wins games. Rather than reacting, he considers the options and thinks through each move. It's not always pretty, but the outcome is all that matters. Nothing is wasted. The old bull never lets testosterone poisoning tempt him to do something just because it makes him look like the baddest guy on the block. He's so confident that he doesn't need to.

In leading, being the old bull is about knowing yourself well enough that you can deploy your genius with discretion, precision, and compassion. Andrew Hayek, the thirty-seven-year-old CEO of Surgical Care Affiliates, is one of the brightest and best young leaders I've ever worked with and a great object lesson for this concept. A summa cum laude graduate of Yale, Andrew and I were introduced when he had just been named the twenty-eight-year-old President and COO of a publicly traded company without having had previous significant leadership experience. Scary smart, though. His boss, a longtime coaching client, suggested Andrew and I get together so I could assist him in his development as a leader. Going in to our first meeting, neither of us was sure exactly where the conversation would go or exactly how I could help him. That unscripted first meeting lasted four hours. As we shook hands to leave, I told him, "There's a huge difference between intellect and wisdom. While you've clearly got an intellectual gift, your ability to grow and demonstrate your wisdom will be the key to creating engaged, committed followers." As coachable as any leader with whom I've worked, he took that wisdom/intelligence distinction to heart. He'll now call me from time to time to tell me that a tough issue came up, one that he might have previously over-reacted to, and shares that he "acted out of wisdom today." It's a wonderful verbal touchstone that translates: *Today, I didn't react. I considered, I responded and I put results first, not what made me feel important.*

Have you ever felt like the old bull—like you achieved more with less effort and more smarts while others were running around in circles? Feels great, doesn't it? You feel like you've solved a puzzle and worked smart, not hard. By contrast, reactionary leading is exhausting, wasteful, and boastful. It is all about jumping to solve a problem and finding a mechanistic cause, employing those warlike business images that we denounced in the last chapter. It's about forcing your intellect into a situation and wrestling the problem to the ground. It's pure ego-driven reaction.

LEADERSH*T
Relying only on developed skills or acquired tools
to qualify oneself as a leader.

LEADING
Understanding the importance of who you are as a person—
character, wisdom and self-knowledge—
and making those qualities central to leading.

Effective leaders keep their streams clear and let their experiences—including their failures—lead them to mindful, self-aware choices. They trust their native wisdom. They do their best to show up powerfully in the present. They suppress their need to self-aggrandize and put their followers in position to shine and take pleasure in their successes. When possible, they don't react. They *respond*.

Self-Protective Behaviors

Outwardly, we appear to be rational beings. We like to think we are. We give to the United Way. We attend symphony concerts and proclaim our love of Shakespeare. However, in the context of geologic time, it hasn't been all that long since we jumped down from the trees and learned to use tools and fill out NCAA basketball tournament brackets. While we may not acknowledge this, our brains know it all too well.

Our rational behaviors sit on top of a base of reactions stemming from events that happened early in our lives. While our brains are still forming, we are trying to survive our families and early experiences from peer pressure to bullying. We develop an array of patterned responses designed to protect us from traumatic events such as abuse, parental conflict, sibling rivalry, abandonment via divorce, unfair expectations, and so on. We carry these patterns with us into adulthood. There's no debate here; we all have them. As the old Ragu commercial said: "It's in there." The patterns are consistent and reliable, and they lie in wait for the stimuli that trigger them.

When someone cuts us off in traffic, we scream an obscenity at the other driver and maybe throw in a gesture for good measure. Later, some of us feel embarrassed and regret flying off the handle. We know you haven't done ourselves any good, but we just couldn't help it. Blind reactions bring out our least praiseworthy and rational qualities.

Such behavior arises from a pea-sized portion of the brain known as the *amygdala*. This is the part of the brain responsible for reactions of fear and rage. When someone or something brushes our emotional triggers, the amygdala sets off a classic "fight or flight" response in our bodies. Adrenaline surges from our adrenal glands, our pupils dilate, our faces flush, and a rush of energy makes it easy to lash out with emotional or even physical violence. It's a primitive response that has nothing to do with reason or choice.

When we are exposed to a triggering event that falls in line with our childhood experiences, our reaction is likely to follow the same pattern that we exhibited when we were children. When I'm fearful, angry, or embarrassed, my response may be to lash out and try to establish my dominance over the other person. Another individual might feign ignorance or powerlessness to defuse the situation. Still another might surrender and placate another person in order to end a conflict. It's a self-protective mechanism. But our brains don't know that we're not still children. Unless we change something, whatever patterned responses worked when we were youngsters will persist into adult (and organizational) life.

The problem is that as adults, those knee-jerk reactions can get us into trouble.

The Drama Triangle

Dr. Stephen Karpman's concept of the "Drama Triangle" illustrates how these situations often play out. According to the Triangle, there are three predictable roles that people without the self-awareness to recognize their patterned responses tend to adopt in reactive situations: Rescuer, Victim, or Persecutor. Rescuers are caretakers who save others. Victims are those who withdraw or allow themselves to be forced to submit, and Persecutors are ruthless aggressors.

The common thread between these three is that they are all totally self-serving. If leaders adopt them, these roles harm productivity and morale because the leader's actions and choices define reality for the followers. Choices that only serve your own primitive emotional needs tell your followers that their needs or the needs of the team or organization don't matter.

LEADERSH*T

Being controlled by ingrained, patterned responses
from childhood that dictate how you react,
as an adult, to certain triggers.

LEADING

Becoming fully aware of those self-protective patterns
and present in the moment when your triggers are
tripped so that you can control your response and
make it affirming and constructive.

This underlines how vital it is for leaders to be aware of their self-protective patterns and learn to make different and wiser choices. Joe Mello is former Chief Operating Officer of DaVita, of one of the most dynamic and successful companies in the healthcare services industry, and he is a tremendous leader. He says, "The only way to lead is to be mindful of every word and action that you take as a leader. Sometimes that means knowing when to say you screwed up and fix it. People watch everything you do and listen to every single word you say. Many times you'll only have the chance to be in front of a group a few times, so even things like whether you look grumpy or happy will help them form their opinions about whether you are the leader or not." Think others didn't see when you reacted with anger or impatience, or that it's no big deal? Joe would disagree.

Want to See Where Wisdom Lives?

Put your hands together in front of you, palms touching. The left is stimulus. The right is response. An effective leader is one who can expand the space between stimulus and response (or slow down automatic reactions) in order to choose the most effective response to a situation. Wisdom—defined earlier as the ability to control one's emotional reactions and allow the right principles, reason, and knowledge to prevail in determining one's actions— lives in that space. Being the old bull is about handling the most challenging situations you face with wisdom (think of its syn- onyms: insight, discernment, and sagacity), which requires con- scious control of your triggers.

Imagine a military commander dealing with an insurgency. A surprise mortar attack on his squadron injures several men and forces his troops to take cover in a bombed-out building. With soldiers bleeding and panicked, the commander has two options. He can surrender to self-protective behavior, express his rage, and send his boys after their attackers without restraint or caution, probably cost- ing many lives. Or he can harness his anger and respond with reason and training—securing the squadron's position, calling in a medical evacuation chopper, and setting up a careful, strategic offensive. If he chooses this option, he probably sustains no more casualties.

As I've said, accessing one's wisdom requires your ability to metaphorically widen the space between stimulus and response—to eliminate that blind, unreasoning reaction to triggers so that experience, judgment, and assessment can drive decision-making. Wise leaders have self-protective behaviors, as do we all. But even when something trips a trigger, they are able to make a speedy transition from reflex to choice, minimizing or preventing damage.

For example, someone schooled in Wisdom Leading might encounter a young staff member who is borderline insubordinate. A less self-aware leader might fly off the handle and deliver a blistering verbal assault on this "young punk," which would accomplish nothing but would temporarily make the leader feel better.

But through a learned discipline and self-knowledge, a leader slows down her natural reactions to insert conscious thought into the interval between the employee's smart-ass comment and the possible angry broadside that might result. By doing so, she will change the outcome of the encounter. Instead of a non-productive outburst, the leader might quickly analyze the character of the employee, see that his youthful bravado masks fear, and choose to assuage the fear. It's not hard to imagine how this would improve rather than damage morale and help develop rather than alienate the young worker.

Fear Itself

The essence of the old bull comes down to stopping and thinking before acting. For many people this means changing the mechanism through which they feel rewarded by leading. Immature leaders might get that sense of reward through dominance. Mature leaders recalibrate the perception of reward and draw pleasure not from a visceral power play over another person *but from the act of responding to stimulus with restraint, fairness and discernment.*

Taking the right action becomes the reward. This is why clients call me and proudly proclaim to have "been the old bull." They know they are rising above their primitive instincts to become finer humans.

It's not easy. I was working with the team at the fall training camp for UCLA gymnastics four months after its 2010 National Championship performance. After a tough day of training, we got this new team together for a session of sharing and talking to set the foundation for the upcoming season. I wanted to insure all athletes got their voices in the room so we could begin creating the container for teamwork.

Right away, some discomfort became apparent among the seniors, who were trying to figure out their places and roles amid a team with such talent, including a very strong freshman class. I let the conversation evolve and the raw feelings come out, because honest and candid expression is typically the way to get to real solutions. At a key moment when things were uncomfortable and reaching a breakthrough in understanding, an assistant coach leapt into an aggressive fire-and-brimstone speech about how nobody was talking about how great it was to be national champions and so on.

It took the air out of the room and in my view was completely inappropriate. Nothing needed to happen at that moment; it would have been perfectly fine to let these young athletes experience the fear and uncertainty they were feeling and learn to resolve it on their own. But the assistant felt uncomfortable and reacted to that discomfort by changing the tenor of the conversation. He was being a classic alpha, unwilling to engage in "soft" talk about feelings and doubts and preferring to cheerlead when he should have demonstrated courage and allowed the uncomfortable vibe in the room to evolve to its logical conclusion.

Fear and threat are the prime drivers of activity in the amygdala, and in leader-follower situations the fear that we may lose control can spark a powerful reaction. We fear being uncomfortable. We fear being forced to face the things that make us afraid. We fear that our pretense will be exposed. Fear is corrosive to any organization. No one can lead through and from fear and be effective.

Awareness, Perspective, Choice

Here are three skills I have found effective in developing the capacity to be a Wisdom Leader:

1. *Awareness.* You're aware that the problem exists because you've read this chapter. Now you need to identify what sets you off and why. What do you react to and how are you protecting yourself by doing so?

2. *Perspective.* This is what I mean by "slowing down the game." Step outside yourself and see the triggered response coming, and do what you must to back it off. Count to ten. Walk around the block. Take twenty minutes and revisit the matter. Research shows that it takes about twenty minutes for your body to clear the epinephrine, cortisol, and other hormones that flood your system under stress, time that allows you to clear your head.

3. *Choice.* Sometimes it's appropriate to be a warrior, but sometimes it's better not to take action. Choosing not to act is an action! The belief that we're not trying unless we're actively manipulating events is wrong. But sometimes nothing is the best thing to do. Lisa Fernandez, arguably the finest softball player ever to lace up cleats, had been programmed during her entire career to act fast and make things happen. As a new assistant coach for UCLA, however, being purely reactive sometimes led her to make big mistakes. Our work together was simply to slow her mind down and act from knowledge—not aggressiveness, fear of mistakes, or adrenaline. Wise leaders turn reflex into choice and, in doing so, gain the power to change outcomes.

Head, Hands, Heart, Spirit

After thirty years at this (and some great teachers), here's what I believe about leading powerfully. It's quite simple. Profound, in fact.

But not easy. When you lead from wisdom, you bring out the best in your followers and produce breakthrough results.

> **LEADERSH*T**
>
> Reacting to stimuli without thinking, often out of fear and often by exhibiting anger, dominance, and other reflexive emotions that make others feel intimidated, insignificant, and disrespected.
>
> **LEADING**
>
> Expanding the time between initial stimulus and your reaction by being fully present and delivering a conscious, chosen response that serves your goals and expands the capacity of your followers.

I often describe this as leading with head, hands, heart, and spirit. The head is your knowledge and strategies. Your hands represent what you can do, your skills and talents, and how you execute those. Your heart stands for empathy and connectedness with others. Spirit is the things you care most about, your passions, and your higher purpose. Powerful, breakthrough leading requires all four. That's rare, because it's hard. They won't come through when you're being the young bull. They won't when you're simply reacting to your triggers. They won't when you're leading on adrenaline. But when you're the old bull, expanding the space between the occurrence of the challenge and your response to it, your head, hands, heart, and spirit can come through loud and clear.

What Are You Playing For?

Let's consider the measure of a great leader. In the end, a leader is only as good as his or her results. The purpose of controlling your reactions to emotional triggers is to expand the capacity of your followers so they will achieve breakthrough results. Anything that doesn't serve that goal is counterproductive.

Wisdom Leading is about figuring out what you're serving. If it's yourself, you're finished before you begin. So . . . what are you playing for?

I'd like you to meet Anna Li, an All-American gymnast whose parents were Olympic gold medalists for China in 1984. She joined the UCLA gymnastics team in 2007, and it became clear over the next three years that she had inherited her parents' talent. However, she's had an up-and-down career because she was emotionally inconsistent on competition days.

Finally, Head Coach Valorie Kondos Field asked Anna, "How do you want to be known? Do you want to be the person who never achieved what she could have?" One of the qualities that make Valorie a great leader is the ability to ask such devastating, thought-provoking questions. Her question rocked Anna to her core.

Early in the 2010 season, the team was struggling on the balance beam, causing their team results to suffer. At a midseason meet, Anna raised her hand and volunteered to go first on the beam. She had never done such a thing before (nor have many other gymnasts, for that matter). In competitive gymnastics, going first on a particular apparatus virtually guarantees you a lower score because the judges want the ability to give higher scores to later athletes. Anna knew this, but she wanted to give the team a strong start in a weak area. She had figured out what she would be playing for from that point in the season: the team, not herself.

She got up and delivered a stellar performance on the balance beam, setting the stage for the entire team. In effect, she was saying, "I'm going to give up the chance to win the NCAA all-around championship so that we can win as a team." Winning the NCAA all-around is the goal of all elite gymnasts, but Anna was acting from essence, not ego.

Well, not only did the UCLA team win that meet, none of its

gymnasts fell off the balance beam *for the rest of the season*. And as you know, they won the NCAA championship again. Anna walked away with a ring and no regrets.

THAT is leading.

LEADERSH*T

Making decisions in order to elevate yourself
or serve your own ego.

LEADING

Making choices that empower your followers
to deliver breakthrough performance
that serves the collective goals of the entire team.

ACCESS POINTS

The Tale of the Old Bull

Questions I've asked myself and others in our journeys to greater wisdom as leaders and in our lives:

What have been the most significant personal lessons I've learned in life?

_____

_____

_____

_____

_____

How did I learn them (e.g., through life's passages, from a particular experience, from others)?

_____

_____

_____

_____

_____

What have I had to let go of in order to make each new step in the
growth of my wisdom?

_____

_____

_____

_____

_____

What is my life's mission or calling?

_____

_____

_____

_____

_____

When I say I am committed to something in life, what does that
mean to me?

_____

_____

_____

_____

_____

Who are the people in my life who know me and my highest purpose and are willing to hold me to my commitments?

_____

_____

_____

_____

_____

What are the most frequent "triggers" that cause me to react to a
situation emotionally?

_____

_____

_____

_____

_____

What are my healthy strategies for slowing down my reactions
when they are triggered?

_____

_____

_____

_____

_____

What's my "haiku" on life and success (simple, short, direct)?

_____

_____

_____

_____

_____

A Final Thought

The attainment of wisdom, typically earned through years of life's triumphs and tragedies, directly correlates with your self-awareness and willingness to learn from it all.

SIX

The Tale of the Trail

Do not go where the path may lead;
go instead where there is no path and leave a trail.
—Ralph Waldo Emerson

hat will make for some interesting walking."

The Wise Man's sarcasm was palpable, but I felt less like cracking wise and more like calling in the Army Corps of Engineers or possibly the guy from Survivorman. Starting at dawn, we had hiked as if our lives depended on it. The weather was perfect, and we were eager to make it to the next decent-sized town down the line. A night of camping in the dampness had intensified my craving for a warm and welcoming tavern, a roaring fire, and a grass-fed steak the size of Delaware. I don't think my companion was far off. Motivated by our animal appetites, we had made twelve miles disappear behind our heels since breakfast.

The wheels in my head had been whirling as I took in the lessons of the past few days. They were all challenging my preconceptions and reshaping what I thought I knew about leading. I found myself mesmerized by the cadence of the old man's speech and the wisdom of his words; he was at times telling me things that I really already know, but he told them in a way that made me finally connect the language with the concrete reality of leading people in my world.

It was exhausting and exhilarating at the same time. Blended with the exertion and the sensory stimulation of trekking through new open country, it was an overwhelming experience that I knew was transforming how I thought and how I would lead.

So I was completely unprepared for the Abyss.

As the morning wore on and the sun became warm and strong, we began doffing layers of clothing to stay cool. The Wise Man led the way up a developed path that had obviously seen the hands of rangers and volunteers. It was marked by reinforcing timbers, drainage culverts, and even a bridge. We snaked up the side of a small mountain, huffing and puffing but rewarded after ninety minutes of rough climbing with a view that stretched at least forty miles to the west. I could see meadows and hills and finally a row of cottonwoods and sycamores that denoted a river. We would follow that river to the town of Adams, where in a couple of days our journey would end and we would part ways.

After a breather, we walked along a level plateau for about half a mile. Abruptly, we came to a set of railroad tracks running at an oblique angle to our course, running off toward the misty blue hills to the northwest. "I think we should follow these tracks," said the Wise Man.

"Really? I think we're making great time on this trail."

"True, but I think this is the old Northern Allegheny line. If I'm right, it would take us only a little out of our way but through some incredible country and over some of the most historic railroad bridges in the state. How about that?" His eyes gleamed.

"Historic" to me meant "old and potentially danger-ous," but I wasn't about to say that to my guide. He hadn't steered me wrong yet, and I was eager to see some rail his-tory. I nodded. "The Northern Allegheny it is," I declared.

"Outstanding!" He jumped onto the tracks and started walking briskly. "Don't fret, Professor. These tracks haven't been used in twenty years. We're perfectly safe."

Famous last words. After an hour of crunching on rail-way gravel as the sun began its slow glide back toward the horizon, I noticed that the trees were thinner. The loam of the northern woods slowly changed to a harder, rockier soil, and granite boulders started popping up like the peaks of buried pyramids. We were climbing into the high country. I welcomed the cooler air but wondered when we would start to descend.

After another hour, as I had fallen about fifty yards behind, I got my answer. My companion suddenly stopped, and I could see him silhouetted against the afternoon sky, his lanky legs slightly bowed. Then I heard him.

"Shit."

I hurried to catch up . . . and kicked gravel over a sheer drop into nothingness.

The Abyss

Clearly, we had found the reason why the Northern Allegheny rail line was no longer in use. Before us stretched a deep-cut canyon at least 200 feet down and maybe half a mile across. At one time a railroad bridge had spanned it, but that was then. Now, the canyon below was strewn with wooden ties, struts, and what could only have been bent steel rails. High wind or perhaps just age had brought the bridge down. An entire historic route possibly dating back to the days of the coal barons had been terminated and no one outside these remote hill towns knew anything about it.

"You know," I offered, "Nietzsche said that when you look into the abyss, the abyss also looks into you."

He glared at me. "Well, right now the abyss is seeing an idiot," he snapped. "Why did I think this line would be intact after all these years? That was dumb." He kicked a stone over the drop; it fell at least 80 feet before clanging against the fender of a rusty car. "If we backtrack, we're going to waste hours."

I looked up and down the rim of the canyon, which

appeared to have been cut by a huge flood many years before. I saw nothing but sheer walls and crumbling dirt. It was absolutely not the type of terrain I cared to negotiate. "Well, maybe we can find a way down and across," I said.

My companion took a deep breath and blew it out, then took off his hat and mopped his brow. As he put the hat back on, I could see him square his shoulders. "Right on, Professor. A little thing like this—okay, a big thing—isn't going to stop us. We'll find a trail down into this mess and out the other side. We've got some time." He began walking and silently waved for me to follow him. We bushwhacked about 100 yards along the southern edge before he stopped me and pointed.

"There," he said.

Running at a forty-five degree diagonal down the face of the cliff was a thin, chalky track that was certainly a superhighway for mountain goats. But for us? I had a better chance of walking on water, I thought.

"There you are," he said. "That trail takes us right down into the canyon, then cuts across the stream and out the other side, you see?" He pointed, and I sighted down his arm to see another spidery trail running up the other bank, which was nowhere near as steep as what we were trying to negotiate.

"I think this might take us down into the canyon a hell of a lot faster than we'd like," I said finally. "I've flossed my

teeth with wider things." If we fell, we'd die. We were miles from anything. But what option did we have? In two hours, we would start losing our light. If this was to be done, it had to be now.

"I think we can make it," he said. "See that outer trail edge? It looks compacted, like people have come through here recently. I don't think it will crumble. If we go slowly and maintain our center of gravity, we can get down." Eyebrows raised, he waited for me to agree or disagree.

Sigh. "Okay, but I'll go first. I'm . . ." I stopped. Sharp as always, he knew what I left unsaid.

"Younger? Yes you are," he said with a grin. "But this was my call. I led you here. And leaders go first. I'll lead the way on this trail, son." He adjusted his pack straps and tied his boots tighter; I did the same, wondering if my life insurance was paid up.

"Ready?" "No."

"Neither am I. Let's go." We stepped into space.

The Descent

The path was not as narrow as it appeared, but it was crumbly as pie crust. With every other step, rocks and soil ran away from under our boots. It was deeply disconcerting. We were both leaning toward the sheer wall to our right, trying to counterbalance the steep pitch of the trail down the wall. I felt like a fly, staying at least ten yards behind my companion so that if I stumbled and went over the edge, at least I wouldn't take him with me.

Conversation? Not on your life. We were both concentrating on left foot, right foot. I watched where the Wise Man set his feet and was careful to place my own feet in the same spots, figuring that he'd packed the dirt a little tighter and made the way a bit safer. In this manner, we inched down the incline, the only sound our own breathing.

Halfway down, he suddenly raised a hand in the manner of those recon leaders you see in movies about patrols in Vietnam. Stop. Now. I stopped. He inched his boot onto the trail directly ahead, ground that appeared to be no different from the collection of dirt and rock we'd already covered. He tapped his boot—and the trail disappeared in a cloud of dust and rocks. At least a foot of the path had vanished, and it would have taken us with it. "I suggest stepping over," he said. "That side has roots running through it, see?" He pointed and I saw thick grass roots swirling through the soil. "Should be safe."

Should be? Before I could say a word, he stepped over the gap—and kept moving. I gulped and followed. We continued downward, taking small, slow steps to keep our centers of gravity stable. Slowly, we approached the tops of the pepper and oak trees that had appeared so small from the high bank. We were going to make it! I checked my watch. We'd have about an hour of good light left, just enough to cross and get up the other side before dusk began to settle over us.

Finally, the bottom was near. I started to let myself gallop, giving in to gravity and the temptation to end my spider walk. I ran up almost on the Wise Man's heels, and he put out a surprisingly strong arm to stop me. "Wait a second, son," he said. "This is the part where we want to be extra careful." He surveyed the trail below. "People at the bottom of a trail like this tend to run and land hard. That can really pack the dirt and make the path slippery. Neither of us wants a broken ankle."

I looked. Nothing about the trail seemed different, but I wasn't about to challenge him. "So what do you suggest?"

He grinned, and then sat and began sliding down the trail. It wasn't dignified, but I'd rather have a dirty back-side than a broken leg. Down I went on my butt to the bottom. When we reached the section about fifteen feet from the floor of the canyon, the trail abruptly steepened and became rock-hard and slippery. If we'd been standing, we'd have been hard pressed not to fall on the sharp rocks below. But eventually, we slid to the bottom, stood, patted the dirt from our pants, and gazed proudly up at the way we'd come.

"Piece of cake," I said.

He looked at me with one eyebrow cocked and strode off to cross the canyon. The scene was surreal: a verdant

streambed strewn with enough hardware to look like a
Mad Max set: wrecked cars, shopping carts, furniture, and
of course the once-proud railway bridge. I walked silently
for a while, but then I had to speak.

"Thank you for leading the way."

He nodded. "Had to," he said. "I charted the course, and
I screwed up. The only thing to do was to take the lead into
the unknown. That's what leaders do."

On our way to the stream, whose gurgling we could
hear, we descended a short hill and skirted a thick pile
of discarded lumber that would make a perfect home for
rattlesnakes. "And you kept us both safe," I said. "That's also
what leaders do."

"Well, it's what they try to do," he replied. "The mistake
a lot of people make on trails like that is thinking they are
bigger than the trail. They think they can conquer it with
their gear, or because they are fit. I once knew a veteran ship
captain who told me that sailing demanded the ultimate
humility, because the ocean could wipe you out of existence
without even noticing. The trail is like the ocean—you don't
conquer it. You survive it based on who you are and how
you think."

Leaders Go First

We had survived our descent because of the Wise Man's
foresight and caution, qualities that were inherent to him.

He'd learned them on his own; he hadn't taken a "How to Avoid Splattering on the Rocks" seminar. We had reached the stream, which was running swiftly with a shimmering sound. It was shallow and we were able to pick our way across in ten seconds, emerging amid railroad ties nearly invisible beneath overgrown gorse and honeysuckle.

"You see, Professor," my companion said as we began picking our way toward the opposite (and not nearly as terrifying) trail on the north wall, "the leader can't just talk. He has to be the one to step into the abyss, to take the big risk before he asks anyone else to do it. Not every leader can do that, but the ones who can don't learn it in business school. It's just part of who they are."

"I see," I said. That was part of the authenticity that I preached to all my clients. Show up fully and deal with the way things are. Be prepared to do everything you are asking your people to do, and do it first. When you do that, the people under you can't help but follow your example. My experience on this afternoon had been a literal example of "walking the walk." Surrender to the circumstances. Be willing to go downhill on your butt. Be humble and honest. Others will come with you.

"Here we are." We had found the opposite trail and immediately began ascending. It was wider and firmer than what we had come down, and it cut a less steep slash up the wall face, which was less than half as tall. Soon, we would be at

the top. "You know," he said as he caught his breath, "I'll bet there's something amazing at the top of this."

"Why?" I asked. "All I saw were trees at the top of this wall."

"Well, I know that when you lead the way into the unknown, there's usually a great reward at the other end," he said, huffing and puffing. "Every time I've taken a big risk or jumped into something inconvenient and daring, I've ended up finding really cool stuff. Haven't you found that to be true?"

Breathing deeply, oddly in sync with the Wise Man, I realized that I had. In my career, each time I had led others into uncharted territory or taken a risk with a big potential payoff, I'd found things I hadn't expected: new relationships, incredible opportunities, and great successes. You lead the way into the abyss, and the wiser you are at picking out a safe trail, the greater the reward on the other end. But nobody would risk it unless you took the first steps. I was reminded of the famous scene in Raiders of the Lost Ark, where Indiana Jones's friend Sallah looks into the snake-filled Well of Souls, claps Indy on the arm, and says, "Asps. Very dangerous. You go first."

"Yes, sir, I have." We pulled our tired bones to the top of the trail, stopped to catch our breath and drink some water, and then ducked between the trees.

Before us lay the Shire from The Lord of the Rings: a

few green hills rolling down to a landscape dotted with farmhouses, neat crops, ponds, and a winding country road that rose and fell prettily until it disappeared around a distant bend. I heard a screen door slam and chickens clucking and saw children playing in a tire swing. I would not have been surprised if Norman Rockwell's brush had appeared in the sky.

"I'd say you were right about that reward," I said to my companion.

"Told you so," he said kindly. He pointed to the southwest, and in the distance I saw the twinkling lights of a village. "There's our destination. I know a fantastic inn with the best organic beef this side of San Francisco."

Movement caught the corner of my eye, and I looked down to the road. "It just got even better," I said. The Wise Man followed my finger to see a public bus bouncing along the road and stopping to pick up an elderly woman standing by her mailbox.

A bus. No walking. I swore I could hear my feet and knees begging softly for mercy.

"I think we can catch it if we run," my companion said. "You up for it?"

"Lead the way." The first stars came out as we let gravity pull us down the hills.

My Thoughts on The Tale of the Trail

In this chapter, I'll discuss my views on the trail leaders blaze by going first. We'll talk about the importance of a leader demonstrating and living the qualities he or she wishes the entire organization to adopt before expecting anyone else to do the same. I'll talk about the need for consistency, the risks in trying to live up to a leader stereotype, and the vital roles of integrity and transparency.

Gandhi said, "We must be the change we wish to see in the world." He didn't say, "We must *do* the change." He knew that before a leader asks anything of her followers, she herself must first be that change. The leader must always be the one to take the first step, lead the way down the dangerous trail, or speak the truth that no one else wants to hear.

Everyone else takes his or her cues from the leader on what is permissible and expected. The leader determines "normal."

To lead her organization through a period of change, a leader must change not what she does but *who she is*. Nothing external matters here—not training, title, education, management style, or raw talent. If you as the leader cannot evolve into the embodiment of the new values or culture you wish to embed in your organization, any hope of change is futile. As I often say, if you want others to be courageous, be courageous; if you want them to be candid, be candid. Nothing's simpler and more powerful in this leading stuff.

Engaging your people, creating a common vision, providing touchstones to determine progress on your journey—these are all useful but in themselves don't constitute leading. Those are outward-focused tactics that have little to do with who you are as a leader. At their worst, they are parlor tricks—cheap substitutes for leaders who cannot or will not show up authentically in the present or critically examine their own choices and responses. Leading is internal. It is about exhibiting your passion, bringing your focus

WISDOM LEADING CONCEPTS

- Leaders go first. They become the change they wish to see in the team, family, or organization

- They are accountable

- Leading means going first, again and again

- Your effectiveness as a leader ultimately rides on the quality of your followers

- You cannot worry about living up to some stereotype of the kind of leader you're "supposed to be"

- Integrity is everything. You can't B.S. or spin people into thinking you have it

WISDOM LEADING GOALS

- Understanding that leading means taking risks before anyone else does

- Making yourself accountable to your followers while maintaining your authority

- Developing a habit of going first, again and again

- Creating strategies that empower your followers to optimize their abilities

- Overcoming worries about being a textbook leader and instead being the leader you were meant to be

- Acting with integrity and adhering to your stated values

to each moment, and applying your energy to leading by example rather than giving rah-rah speeches and holding meetings.

LEADERSH*T

Handing change down from on high, like Moses.

LEADING

Being the first to engage in the change, often at personal risk.

I have witnessed incredible cultural and personal turnarounds in organizations where leaders have the courage to truly be themselves, often for the first time in a professional setting. When they admit their weaknesses and failings and exhibit the character to reveal how they will face their own challenges, the entire corporate dynamic shifts. When the leader becomes vulnerable, it creates a "safe zone" in which everyone feels free to drop their own façades, admit their fears and worries, and move on to a shared spirit of working together to change things.

Leading Never Stops

Leadership: noun. Leading: verb. One, static. The other, active. The words reflect the reality. Leading is a fluid, evolving enterprise. Executives new to the concept of Wisdom Leading often have a difficult time with this, and this has bred one of the more common misconceptions about leading: that going first one time is enough to change the entire culture.

It is not. Few single actions, no matter how dramatic, will linger in the consciousness of the led beyond a short time. Leading never stops. As a leader, you must be the first to take culture-shifting action and then *continue* taking similar actions. Cultural inertia is a powerful force within any organization; habits are hard to kill.

If you do not constantly support a new direction with continued action, habits will reassert themselves. There is no point at which you can say, "Well, I've led. I'm good."

This is why having an attitude of personal transformation is so crucial and why I drive that home with such force. If you attempt to remake your organization's culture without genuine shifts in how you think, feel, and show up, what you do will be *unsustainable*. If the change isn't in you, it won't take.

Some other truths about the "leaders go first" concept:

• *Change your story.* The story you tell yourself about yourself is part of your reality. "I can't tackle that crisis" is fundamentally different from "I may be nervous about handling it, so I'll summon the troops and figure out how we will tackle it." If you are to lead authentically and powerfully, start telling a different story about yourself and recognize the power of your words to frame reality for you and others. As former IBM president Thomas J. Watson said, "Nothing so conclusively proves a man's ability to lead others as what he does from day to day to lead himself."

One of the most potent examples of this is the journey of Starbucks chairman and CEO Howard Schultz. Schultz left his position in 2000 after overseeing the company's incredible expansion into virtually every corner of the globe. But he saw it becoming a faceless franchise instead of operating like a small company, a characteristic that had always been part of his vision.

So in 2008, Schultz resumed his duties as chairman and CEO, accepting responsibility for the cultural changes that had negatively impacted Starbucks. Schultz could have left well enough alone and maintained his personal story as "the man who built Starbucks," but he chose to take responsibility. His story became "My leadership made the company lose focus on what is really important." Under his new governance, the company has closed outlets, made efforts to improve its products, opened community feedback channels, redesigned its coffee shops to be more in keeping with local styles, and engaged in more green initiatives. Love it or hate it, Starbucks would not have undertaken these huge changes without Schultz's new personal story, which wrote a new story for his company.

• *Don't wait for crisis.* Howard Schultz did not wait until Starbucks was in danger of going out of business. Other leaders cannot make the same claim. Blockbuster was once the titan of home video rentals, with about 60,000 employees at its peak in 2009. But as Netflix and other online video companies began to cut into its profits, the company's leadership made a series of disastrous decisions. In 2007 it named James W. Keyes as the new chairman and CEO; rather than use the company's financial muscle to build a viable online alternative to Netflix, Keyes decided to double down on the failing retail environment.

But consumers had already spoken. They wanted convenient online video availability, and Blockbuster's attempts to expand its brick and mortar footprint looked stubborn and misguided. In 2010, Blockbuster filed for Chapter 11 bankruptcy and continues to close stores. By the time the company's leaders chose to act, their solutions had become totally obsolete.

Effective leaders do not wait for crisis. Crisis demands more drastic action to right the ship, and it's always more difficult to get employees to buy into radical solutions. Great leaders know it's better to have high standards for an organization, be observant, and take action when the organization begins to fall short of those standards—NOT when the ship is taking on water. A revolution works better when followers don't even realize that it's necessary.

• *Expect pushback.* No matter how charismatic or wise you are, you will find that some people don't want to change the status quo. This is another reason why "leaders go first" is so powerful: it reveals which follower is playing by his own rules, not yours. This gives you the knowledge to clear that obstacle in your stream.

> **LEADERSH*T**
> Thinking a single, powerful act of leading
> is sufficient and waiting for a crisis to take action.
>
> **LEADING**
> Renewing your story, being proactive,
> and anticipating pushback from entrenched interests.

The Measure of Leading

One of my favorite Warren Bennis quotes (and one I've used previously in this book) is that the leader and the led are intimate allies. I agree. Your effectiveness will be most visible in the way that those you lead respond to your taking the first step. You can determine how you show up, coming to each situation fully present and engaged. But beyond that, you are powerless, like an actor or other artist, doing his or her best work and then submitting it for the public's verdict. The actor who's just finished playing Richard III doesn't decide whether he deserves a standing ovation. The audience does.

This is one of the reasons that leading is lonely. Most CEOs, parents, and coaches experience occasional feelings of isolation in their work, because no matter how many colleagues they have, no one bears the same responsibilities they do. I often think that half of the value of what I do is not in coaching but in just being a neutral party who listens. Leaders know they can unload on me, ask my honest opinion without blunting their authority, and get useful feedback untainted by flattery.

Each leader is at the center of a delicate balance. He or she sets the example but does not decide the outcome. Followers grant (or deny) the leader authority just as the Declaration of Independence describes government's power as deriving from the consent of the governed. But the led don't have the power to create policy or make decisions. Each party depends on the other for its full expression. Without the led, the leader has no one to lead. Without a leader, the led become a mob.

Most important of all, your actions must be congruent with who you have represented yourself to be. Otherwise, you risk being labeled a hypocrite and a phony, and that will cost you your followers. As Ralph Waldo Emerson said, "What you do speaks so loudly that I cannot hear what you say."

The Leader You're Supposed to Be

Matt Brubaker, my business partner and colleague at The Foster Mobley Group, says, "The average leader spends at least 20 percent of his time each day trying to be the leader he is *supposed* to be rather than the leader he is." This is a brilliant insight. Many of us have in our minds a template of what the leader of an organization is supposed to be: steely in resolve, visionary, iron-willed, disciplined, passionate, intellectually brilliant, and personally charismatic.

The point is that no one can live up to our culture's mental picture of the perfect leader any more than a boxer can be the perfect replica of Rocky Balboa. Some leaders try and inevitably fall short, which undermines their confidence and breeds the fear that they will be discovered as failures. Trying to match the perfect leader stereotype is exhausting. More than that, it's inauthentic. It erodes trust, because nothing is more transparent than someone trying to be something he's not.

This is why it's so critical to show up as the person you are and to lead from that honest place. When you lead from authenticity, you will have authentic allies. If I know who you are, and you say what you are committed to, I will run through fire for you. If we have a non-intimate relationship—logical, rational, but based on fear instead of passion and shared meaning—I will work just hard enough not to get fired. As the late W.L. Gore said, "Commitment, not authority, produces results." You must be real, honest, and open to gain that deep, lasting commitment.

LEADERSH*T

Posturing and leading from image, expectations, or fear.

LEADING

Showing up authentically and being the person you are, instead of the leader you think you should be, committed to leading by example.

What Is Integrity?

No one ever takes a risk expecting to fail.

Think about it. Do you bet on the roulette wheel in Las Vegas expecting to lose your money? Of course not. Do you go scuba diving saying to yourself, "Well, this is the time I get eaten by a great white shark, c'est la vie"? I hope not. When we take risks, even extreme risks, we always believe that somehow we will come out on top. Sometimes, this belief is utterly delusional (I return you to the Vegas gaming tables as an example), but it's still there.

As a leader, you are the spearhead of risk. That's your job. You initiate change and innovation. If a calculated risk pays off, you enjoy the bulk of the rewards. If it bombs, you take the brunt of the damage. It comes with the territory. When the organization jumps into risky territory, your neck is automatically on the chopping block.

Here's the key thing to remember: sometimes, your long-shot horse will finish last. When that happens, integrity means accepting responsibility for that failure. In going first, you will fail on occasion. It's inevitable. The failure isn't what sinks leaders; it's their responses. It's not the scandal, as they say; it's the cover-up.

When you respond from ego, either refusing to take responsibility or becoming defensive, then you are more likely to find yourself disgraced and terminated. The chief executive graveyard is littered with the careers of formerly high-flying men and women who could not face failure.

Wise leaders swallow hard and face failed bets with humility and integrity. They know that sometimes shit happens and you can't take it personally. They also know that a failure can be a great opportunity for a personal and organizational reboot—a wake-up call from complacency.

You can see the difference by contrasting two corporate titans' responses to massive failures. Cisco Systems had a market cap of $500 billion in 2000, but when the dot-com bubble exploded, it took $250 billion of that corporate value with it. It was devastating. CEO John Chambers didn't wallow in grief or point fingers. He took decisive, difficult action to save his company—enacting layoffs, restructuring Cisco, and putting the brakes on its binge of acquisitions. His actions saved the company.

Then we have BP, formerly British Petroleum. You don't need me to tell you what an unmitigated disaster the Deepwater Horizon oil spill still is for the people of the Gulf Coast. But from the beginning, as oil gushed into the Gulf of Mexico, CEO Tony Hayward dodged and ducked, doing ridiculous things like calling the spill "relatively tiny" compared to the size of the ocean. But on May 30, 2010, he drove the stake into his own heart when he said, "There's no one who wants this thing over more than I do. I'd like my life back." In coming across as narcissistic and self-involved, Hayward doomed himself. He left the company that October. BP, meanwhile, lost a huge amount of its value and continues to struggle.

You are the moral center of your organization or family. What you consider ethical becomes the group's ethics. When you combine ethics with authenticity of words and action, you get *integrity*. The first dictionary definition of this word is "steadfast adherence to a strict moral or ethical code," but it's the second that's the attention getter: "the quality or condition of being whole or undivided." Your integrity in the face of risk takes the separate individuals of your organization and unites them.

The strength of the relationship between leader and led depends on the integrity of who you say you are and what you do. Are you consistent and predictable in adhering to your morals and ethics? If so, you likely have many willing followers who feel comfortable being authentic themselves. They will deliver breakthrough results for you, in part out of respect and gratitude for that freedom.

If you don't act from integrity, your people probably go through the motions in their work or don't even stick around. Think about a building: If it lacks integrity, do you feel comfortable in it? No. You head for the exit at the first opportunity. When you're the leader, there's no place to hide. You either are who you say you are or you aren't.

Beware the Bullshit Detector

If you want to lead with authenticity and passion, then act according to the values and ethics that are most important to you. Are you all about customer service? Great. Time with your family? Fine. There are no wrong answers here as long as you are true to what moves you in your heart of hearts. Admit it and then back it up with action.

Above all don't attempt to "spin" truth. It can't be done. We still try to do it because we fear accountability, but it never works. Americans are cynical; after watching so many television news broadcasts that try to manipulate our fears and desires, we've become great at knowing bullshit when we see it. You can't fool people's bullshit detectors.

Think about Toyota. That company looked unstoppable. It grabbed the title as number one automaker in the world from GM and looked poised to dominate the future. But when its cars started having well-publicized problems with sudden acceleration, the company dodged and deflected rather than facing the issues head-on. The impact was disastrous. Because it favored spin over integrity, Toyota is no longer the number one seller of cars in the U.S., and Ford will probably overtake it as number two.

Spin your followers and you turn them into cynics. If you respect the led enough to share the facts and frame them in a way that defines reality, without denying challenges, you will win respect. In the end, nothing you say will change a preexisting bias in an organization. You can only change it by courageous action that's consistent with who you say you are and stand for. Talk is cheap. Walking that steep trail is what gets you where you're going.

LEADERSH*T

Spinning the facts in order to manipulate people
into believing what you want them to believe.

LEADING

Respecting followers by giving them truth and
acting on the facts in a way that's congruent
with your stated values.

ACCESS POINTS

The Tale of the Trail

Questions I've asked myself and others in our in our work to be the kind of leaders who go first and act with integrity unifying our words and actions:

When do I act courageously in support of my beliefs or commitments? When do I not?

_____

_____

_____

_____

_____

When I don't act courageously in support of what I believe or want, what is holding me back?

_____

_____

_____

_____

_____

What is the difference I want to make in the world?

_____

_____

_____

_____

_____

In what ways are my current actions and priorities consistent or inconsistent with that commitment?

_____

_____

_____

_____

_____

Where do I most often fall short of my commitments to others? To myself?

_____

_____

_____

_____

_____

When I overpromise or overcommit, what need in me is that serving?

_____

_____

_____

_____

_____

In what areas is my life a testament to what I say and believe is important? Where is it not?

_____

_____

_____

_____

_____

A Final Thought

I'm constantly guided by a prayer I learned in Kenya a few years ago: "There's no use praying unless we pray with our feet."

SEVEN

The Tale of the Spring

The willingness to accept responsibility for one's own life
is the source from which self-respect springs.
—Joan Didion

*T*he closing day of our time together began uneventfully.
From this tiny, bucolic village we would continue our hike
west, intersect with a river, and then follow it downstream
to Adams, where we would pass the night in conversation
and part ways the following morning—I back to Califor-
nia, my companion back to wherever his fancy took him.

The Wise Man pounded on the door of my room
obscenely early, shaking loose both some dust from the
ceiling and a few choice curse words from me. The prior
day's descent into the canyon had left my knees and
ankles barking at me, and I wasn't eager to shoulder
my pack again and hit the trail for what promised to be
another twelve-mile day, even knowing that things would
loosen up once I warmed up.

"Rise and shine, Professor!" he bellowed. "Got a big day

ahead of us! Get yourself vertical, chop-chop!" I groaned, pulled myself upright, showered, shaved, and dressed, and by the time I got downstairs to meet my far-too-chipper guide, I was feeling marginally human. A big mug of coffee helped.

"No steep climbs today, buddy," he said, clapping me on the shoulder. "We're on flat ground today. Shouldn't be any surprises."

I grinned at him. "You realize you just said the magical surprise-inducing incantation, right?" I said. He rolled his eyes. After the subtle, unexpected things we had run across during our first six days on the road together, a quiet day would be welcome, but it was unlikely. I finished my coffee, handed over my room key, hefted my much lighter pack (we were almost out of food), and followed him out into the growing sunlight.

The inn was on a hill above the village, and from the elevation of its front yard we surveyed the day's route. As the light increased, I could see the trail snaking out of town and over a series of mild hills that would be easy walking. Eventually, we would intersect a dark green shadow on the horizon: the line of woods that marked the river, which would lead us to the small town that was our final destination. It looked inviting, and I said so.

"Yep, should be a great day," my companion said brightly. "You ready?" I was. We crunched down the gravel driveway

in the great silence of the early morning, and our last day together got underway.

A mile out of town, the whaleback section of the trail began: rising, falling, and then rising like a children's roller coaster. A fresh breeze carried the scent of pine and tilled earth from the north and dried the sweat on our faces, making the walking much more pleasurable. The terrain was unremarkable, and after an hour riding the mild thrill ride of the trail hillocks, I decided to break the silence.

"Tell me something," I said.

My companion didn't pause in his stride but turned his head to the left to indicate he heard. "Fire away."

"How much time do you spend doing this, hiking from town to town in the backcountry?"

He appeared to think for a moment, and while he did a huge red-tailed hawk soared overhead, clearly on the hunt. I saw it dart abruptly downward into a field, and when it didn't reappear immediately, I knew it had found a meal. Finally, the Wise Man said, "I suppose I spend five or six months a year doing this."

My eyebrows lifted. "Why?"

This time he turned to face me, walking backward effortlessly. "Well, as you might have guessed, I'm retired. I used to be a schoolteacher. When I retired, I decided to be a part-time nomad." He grinned. "I also found that I meet a lot of interesting people when I'm in the wild," he said, nodding at me. "Being out here is my source."

"Your source?"

He seemed to sense that a tree was jutting out into the trail and turned on his heel to face forward again, neatly sidestepping the roots that might otherwise have tripped him. "My source of energy, of power. It's what keeps me going the other six or seven months of the year when I can't be out here because of the weather or other obligations."

He shot a look over his shoulder again. "What about you, Professor? What's your source?"

I didn't have an answer for that one. He shrugged and kept walking, but I fell back a bit as my mind went into overdrive. What kept me charged up and doing what I did? What kept leaders in general going, taking on major challenges and fighting endless battles while keeping their values in front of them?

"Maybe this last day will help you figure it out," said my companion, now about twenty yards ahead. "Be a shame not to know what keeps you going."

Swimming Upstream

We tramped on, leaving the roller coaster behind for a deep-cut track that ran among hollyhocks and rhododendrons bigger than anything I had ever seen. Apparently, they thrived in the fertile soil; they dwarfed us and made *me feel like a character in a children's storybook. Stopping for lunch in the shade of an enormous oleander plant, the Wise Man and I chatted about this and that while my mind whirled around the question about my source. I wondered if I would find the answer before my time with this fascinating man ticked away.*

After lunch my pack was pleasantly light, as much of its remaining weight now resided in my belly, and we set off at a brisk pace through the narrow alley of overgrowth. Finally, we emerged at the top of an alluvial ridge.

"There's the river." My guide pointed, and as I sighted along his arm I could see the distant sparkle of running water about a mile and a half distant. It was one thirty; we were making excellent time. He set off again and I followed, eager to reach the water. But after about twenty minutes of rapid walking, he slowed, then stopped.

"What is it?" I asked. He was peering at the ground alongside the trail, which had widened into a sparsely vegetated fire road. Alongside it ran what looked like a ditch about four feet wide and three deep, and this was where his gaze fell. His furrowed brow betrayed concern.

"This," he said, pointing at the ditch, "is a seasonal stream. Normally, this time of year it would be filled with frogs and water hyacinths and fish, but look . . ." I stepped over and to be sure, the stream was virtually empty. No frogs, no fish. There was barely enough water to moisten the ground.

"Another blockage?"

He shook his head. "I don't know. I've been through this area several times at this time of year, and this stream has always been rollicking with life. I was looking forward to hearing the frogs chirp while we walked. I don't know what to make of it." He tapped his grizzled chin with two fingers as he thought. Then his right index finger shot skyward. "But I know how to find out." And with that, he leaped across the streambed like an antelope and walked at a fast clip back the way we had come.

I just stared for a moment. "What are you doing?"

He waved me on. "Going to the springs! Get with it!"

I wasn't feeling terribly antelope-like, so I carefully stepped through the dry watercourse and up the other bank, then trotted to catch up to him. "I suspected we'd run into some sort of surprise," he said, panting as we hiked uphill. "That's been one of the fun things about this trip, Professor: you seem to bring out the unexpected in Mother Earth." He laughed, and I joined him.

We were following the distinct cut of the streambed as it ran east and then turned north into rocky, low hills. "This stream was diverted when the fire road was built, but before that it was a natural tributary of the river we'll see later," he said. "It's fed by springs that surface in those rocks up there." He pointed to some step-like outcroppings about another quarter-mile above us. "They should feed the *stream year-round, which is why I don't understand this. But it's a great opportunity for one more discussion."*

We huffed and puffed our way uphill. As we drew closer to the rocks, I could make out the faint trickling sound of running water. Climbing up between a stand of jutting boulders, we finally emerged among a series of tiered pools. At their head, a flow of clear water ran from a hole in the rocks down into one pool, then the next, then the next, and on into another dark tunnel in the stone. The Wise Man dropped his pack and bathed his face in the rivulet of water. I did the same and was shocked by its coldness. It was like being hit in the face with a snowball in August.

"This is it," he said, peering around at the flat, sun-drenched rock plateau. "This is the spring that feeds that stream and eventually the river. It's the source of all that downstream life. It's good to see it running strong and healthy."

"But then why was the stream dry?" I asked, taking a seat on the warm stone, feeling the heat bake through my clothes.

"I'm not sure," he admitted. "This spring is fed by the local aquifer and runs year-round. It should be recharged by all the rain we've had. There doesn't seem to be anything blocking it—" he pointed down to where the water vanished into its underground course on its way downhill—"so it should be reaching the stream where we were." He pushed

himself up the hill a bit farther, above the headwaters, to survey the land. I sat and watched the water run. It was hypnotic. I thought about my own source of replenishment and how it seemed to ebb and flow naturally, as this one did. Can we always be "on," at the top of our games as human beings and leaders? Or do we need those times when things don't flow to remind us to keep striving and asking questions?

My companion came back down the hill. "I don't understand it," he said. "This is the only source for that stream."

A thought hit me. "Tell me," I began, "before we started this hike, had it been raining a lot in this area?"

His weathered face scrunched together as he thought, standing over me like a scarecrow. "No," he said finally. "As a matter of fact, it hadn't rained for about three weeks before I met you, a long time for this area in June." His eyes sparkled. "You think that's the answer?"

I stood. "I think so. You said this source runs all the time, year round. But if there was a brief drought, then it would have slowed, and the ground would have dried out. So maybe there's no water downstream because since the rains came, the ground upstream is absorbing all the moisture." The talk of water made me thirsty and I drank from my bottle. "I'll bet if we came back here in a week or ten days, we'd see plenty of water in the stream."

He slapped his leg, then came over and slapped me just

as hard on the back. "I think you're right!" He led me over to the place where the water disappeared into the rocks after it left the lowest tiered pool. "See, the water reenters the earth here and flows for about a quarter mile downhill before it comes back out from underground. But it could easily be filling spaces down there that have never seen the light of day, reservoirs that ran dry when there was no rainfall. Once those pools fill, they'll spill over and the water will rush downstream."

I watched as a small fish swam into the dark crevice along with the water, riding its own version of Splash Mountain. "This is like your source, isn't it?" I said. "It might slow a little when you can't be on the road, but it's always running."

He smiled. "That's true for everyone, son. We all have a source of energy that keeps us going. When you're the leader, your spring is feeding everyone else. If your source isn't strong and sure enough, the water runs dry and you lose your people.

"Values, play, meaning, physical vitality—those are all sources that motivate us, bring us joy, and keep us going when the road gets hard," he continued. There are as many sources, as many different springs, as there are people." His eyes twinkled in the strong sunlight, and for the first time I realized that he never wore sunglasses. "You figure out what your source is yet?"

I shook my head.

He smiled gently and slid his pack down to the rock. "What it is doesn't matter. The only thing that matters is having a source and keeping it flowing, ready to be tapped." He walked over to the rock dome above where the spring gurgled from under the ground and abruptly sat down. "That's the trick: being wise enough to tap that spring and drink deep."

"What are you doing?"

He assumed a cross-legged position. "I'm saying a prayer of thanks for the spring," he said. "You don't have to stay. I'll be a few minutes." He placed his hands on his knees and closed his eyes.

I didn't move a muscle. The warm, reverent silence of this spot was overwhelming. After a minute, I sat back down on the warm stone and watched him utter his silent prayer. I assume he was chanting in his mind in some Native American tongue, but he never made a sound. What happened was between him, the rock, the spring and the sky. I was a spectator, honored to be present.

And To the Last

After a few minutes, he opened his eyes and placed his hands palms down on the warm rock, smiling as if offering a benediction. Then without a word he stood, walked over to his pack, shouldered it, and hustled back down the way we had come. Flustered, I grabbed my gear and kicked up a cloud of dust trying to keep up.

"That's it?" I asked.

"That's it," he said. "Our business here is done. Time to move on." He grinned a joyous grin.

I often saw a hint of that same joy in the faces of some of the people I coached, the ones who "got it." Despite the pressures of their duties, they found ways to let their springs flow in their lives. Whatever animated them and got them to work each morning with fire in their eyes, they embraced it. They considered it just as important as they considered their work—or more. Because of that, their batteries were usually charged. Their lives weren't perfect, but they were as rich, deep, and full of vitality as the stream

I followed the Wise Man down the hill and back to the trail without really seeing the terrain we walked over. So I was surprised when his shout pulled me back to the present: "There she is!" We stood above a swift, cool river. Spruce, pine and willow trees lined its banks, and I could see the handprint tracks of a raccoon in the mud below where we stood. The air was fragrant. I felt that I was close to something.

"Not bad." My guide closed his eyes and inhaled. Then he tapped my pack, walked past me, and headed south-ward along a riverfront trail.

The rest doesn't bear much retelling: we meandered for

another two hours through water oaks and sycamores, watched a beaver trolling upstream with a stick in its teeth, and listened to the wind in the trees. All the while I felt slightly mournful, knowing that the trek was coming to a close, but I also felt exultant. I had made a friend and had my eyes opened. I'd had a wonderful experience that I knew would leave me changed forever.

Eventually, the trail led us to a side street in the town of Adams, a nice, two-stoplight place with tidy houses on quiet streets. We fell into our usual town rhythm: rooms at a local inn, showers, dinner and beers at the local tavern, and lots of deep conversation. That night, we listened to an Irish combo—harp, fiddle, guitar, and drum—play until the wee hours.

The following morning, I rose feeling drowsy; we'd stayed up very late. After dressing and stretching, I came down to the common room to find it empty. I asked the desk clerk if my older friend had come down yet, and she said kindly, "Oh, he checked out about two hours ago and vanished. He said to give you this." She handed me an envelope, and I sat down at one of the long tables. No goodbye, which was somehow appropriate. He'd vanished as quickly as he'd come.

I slid the envelope flap open, took out the single sheet of paper, and read what was written on it in compact, graceful handwriting:

Professor,

I had to make my way to the next stop along my trail, so our path together ends here. It was an honor sharing time and trail with you and discovering the truth of things in a blocked stream, an empty house, a quiet lake lined with stones for skipping. Thank you for listening to an old man's wanderings; listening is as much a gift as speaking and tends to teach a great deal more. I'll remember our time together, and I leave you with this: you already know what your spring is. That's why you're so damned good at helping other people find theirs.

May your trails always lead to wonders. Adios.

—S.

S. That was as much as I would ever know about his identity. But I had so many questions! Where would he go next? What did he know about my spring that I didn't know? What had he done in his life to make him regard everything with such serenity and acceptance? Why—

Then it hit me. Of course. I laughed softly, and the desk clerk looked up. It must have been obvious to him, and now it was obvious to me. Questions. It was the questions that were my source, my spring. Not answers but the finding of answers in human behavior, social psychology, sports—you name it. Questions got me up in the morning, animated my days, and filled me with purpose. That was it. I didn't want someone to show me the spring running in the sunlight; I wanted to see the dark tunnel where the water goes and figure out where it winds up.

Questions. Mine and those of the leaders I coached and counseled. My innate sense of curiosity—my passion for exploration—was my spring. It would never stop running as long as I kept asking questions, because no one has all the answers. Not even a strange, wise gent trucking toward another town, another inn, or perhaps, finally, a ride home for the season.

I nodded my head in thanks. Fishing in my pack, I drew out the hiking hat I'd worn during our trip together. I set in on the table and leaned the letter against it. It wasn't mine to keep, and anyway, I would never forget a word of it. Let others find it and ask their own questions.

I checked out and paid my bill. Feeling wistful, I walked into the streets of the awakening town to find breakfast and then a bus that would take me toward home.

My Thoughts on The Tale of the Spring

In this chapter, I will close by talking in greater detail about the concept of the Source, the wellspring of energy and purpose that keeps us all going. I will discuss the roles passion and values play in fueling our desire to lead, and the importance of taking back personal time without guilt. Finally, I will talk about the roles that joy and happiness play in the development and maintenance of great leaders, and the importance of understanding why we make the choices we make.

ISDOM LEADING CONCEPTS

- You have a source that gives you the energy and passion to lead, and your source is different from everyone else's

- Your values should direct your choices as leader

- Do not ignore the necessity of personal time and its recharging effects on mind and body

- You deserve to love your work

- Your essence is who you are when you are at your best

- Everything begins with understanding "why." Never stop asking questions

ISDOM LEADING GOALS

- Understanding what your source is and how to replenish it

- Knowing what your core values are and how they affect your decisions and your your followers

- Retaking your personal time without guilt

- Putting happiness and satisfaction with your life's course above all other gauges of success

- Leading from essence, not ego

- Figuring out the right questions to ask

We are also at the end of our time together. How fitting that we should do it by returning to the concept that's closest to my heart: the stream. Early on in my coaching work with a client, after I discuss clearing blocked streams, I don't ask the next logical question: *How do you sustain your stream?* Frankly, for most of us, the greatest, fastest lift comes from simply clearing the stream and letting it run free. But in the end, we have to come back to the source.

Effective leaders who aspire to create breakthrough results with a team of inspired, fully engaged followers must first fully engage their entire beings in the act of leading. *Leading and being cannot be separate.* We don't put on our leader hats when we leave our houses in the morning and take them off when we pull out of our parking spaces in the evening. Leading must be part of the skin you're in.

My metaphorical journey through the backcountry was a way of illustrating that leading—the fundamental principles that are its bastions and pillars—is everywhere. The concepts of meaning, the flow of energy, the power of tuning out distracting noise, and the wisdom of the old bull exist in many places and situations. Leading is organic, not something to be gleaned from seminars and Power-Point presentations.

As you now know, the stream represents everything that runs through us to our organization and its people when we are functioning fully—ideas, enthusiasm, presence, openness, risk taking, and more. Blockages in that stream—arising from stress, fear, doubt, noise, disempowering stories, or limiting beliefs—keep us from functioning optimally and bringing everything that we can to the table. But where does the stream begin? Something compels us to get up each day, get moving, and write a few more pages in the story of our lives. Those forces are the *source* for everything that flows from us.

The forces that are our source have little to do with business. They affect our performance in the professional sphere but rarely originate there. Purpose, joy, family, engrossing interests, moving experiences—they resemble underground power lines that we tap to give us what we need to show up, be fully present for our people, and do what needs to be done. Like the spring in this last story, our sources can run dry if we neglect them—something that's all too easy in today's high-pressure world.

Keeping your source fully charged with inspiration, joy, and challenge may be the single most important step you can take to ensure the longevity of your role as a leader.

The Value of Values

"You gotta serve somebody," says Bob Dylan, and he's right. I was raised as a person for whom serving others was the highest calling. To this day, service remains one of my core values. With all of my clients, I'm focused on one question: How can I serve them with the greatest positive effect? I will labor for hours to do something meaningful for someone else and not even notice the time passing. I'll work all night and into the sunrise without fatigue. I imagine that you've felt the same thing when you've been involved with your favorite charity or helping a friend.

Contrast this with what happens when you're engaged in a task where the work doesn't have an aspect of service. I'm tired by dinnertime if I'm doing that. We were built to serve. I believe we are at our best when we're given the chance to aid our brothers and sisters. We rise to heights of selflessness and nobility that we otherwise don't approach. Gandhi said, "The best way to find yourself is to lose yourself in the service of others."

Service is one of the most powerful values you'll find in the world of business. Others include charity, justice, and equality—concepts that, when expressed fully, improve the lives of others and humanity as a whole. Whatever values matter most to you, when you are connected to them at the deepest level and bring them into your work, you are plugged into another important source of power.

Most great leaders I work with are idealists at some level, shaped by their values. Whether you value the environment or literacy, local economies or the arts, social justice or healthy families, living and leading as an expression of your values can infect everyone around you with your enthusiasm. Work becomes meaningful and purposeful. There's pride and accomplishment in something greater than oneself. Values can give you—and by virtue of your position, your followers—something that any organization finds priceless: a genuine mission.

LEADERSH*T

Serving only the daily agenda in your professional life—
hunkering down and getting through.

LEADING

Serving a set of idealistic values that
you pass on to your people,
infusing your organization with
a soaring sense of personal mission.

Personal Time without Guilt

Business can be draining. At an elite level, it demands everything of you—passion, intellect, endurance, foresight, and of course, endless time to complete tasks that seem immense. It's no wonder that so many people suffer from burnout. Business can be a harsh mistress. For many executives, the remedy is simple but neglected: take care of your body, mind, and spirit so that you can replenish your physical, emotional, and spiritual energy.

We derive much more than actual motive energy from exercise, meditation, or whatever turns us on. We derive a sense of well-being and control. Sadly, even for those in the C-suite, defending their precious bubbles of limited personal time is like defending a fortress that's under assault from all sides. There are people who would gladly sacrifice your health on the altar of their share prices. Yet for effective leaders, self-care is absolutely critical. We can't lead with empty tanks. Believe me, I've tried!

Dick Eaton is a longtime friend and colleague and the founder of Leapfrog Innovations, which designs experiential learning simulations for corporations. He has a lot to say about this broken paradigm. "People aren't in the office now, but they are expected to be connected to work as their primary life force, no matter where they are," he says. Many corporate cultures don't acknowledge the psychological need for personal time, and if you don't create those boundaries for yourself, you'll feel pressure to respond even when you are on vacation or with their kids or at dinner.

"You need to model the way that you want your organization to behave," he continues. "People are even more expected to do more now in this economy—they feel more pressure to be on call all the time. There is more work to be done and businesses haven't added people. Can you spend your people to get it all done? How do you walk your talk?"

Dick knows that people who carve out personal time for themselves have more productive time at work, less sick time, less absenteeism, and less "presenteeism." They enjoy themselves more and, as a result, they perform in a superior fashion. When we're working, we're moving at a hundred miles an hour, with 3 a.m. GoToMeeting conference calls in Switzerland, days of meetings scheduled fifteen minutes apart, and relentless deadlines. We're charging hard, and technology lets us cram more into our workdays than ever. Today's leaders need *more* rest and revitalization, not less.

If you want personal time and the uninterrupted freedom to work out, pursue a hobby, or do anything else that refills your spring and keeps your stream flowing, you're going to have to fight for it. Even if you are the CEO, business culture dictates that the needs of the many (the company and its shareholders) outweigh the needs of the few (you).

This is a mistake. As the leader, you benefit many when you are fully present and courageously open and honest, with the endurance to put in long days and still be as effective at 8 p.m. as you were at 5 a.m. If you don't serve yourself first, you will be unable to serve other people.

Become the change you hope to benefit from. Initiate new, more sustainable policies regarding personal "recharge" time, and they will flow downstream to everyone else. I can't imagine an employee balking at being given permission to *not* answer his cell phone on a weekend or to take an hour each day to exercise. This sort of cultural revolution will spread quickly once it starts, but you have to be the one to initiate it.

LEADERSH*T

Letting yourself and your people be drained dry
by constant work demands and a culture
that does not tolerate self-care or disconnected time.

LEADING

Refilling your spring by turning off your BlackBerry
from time to time, allowing yourself to care for
body and mind without guilt,
and giving those under you approval to do the same.

Enjoy Your Work? Why Not?

My goal in life is to unite my avocation with my vocation, as my two eyes make one in sight. For only where love and need are one, and work is play for mortal stakes, is the deed ever really done, for heaven's and for future's sake. —Robert Frost

The greatest source of recharge for those mental and physical batteries is taking pleasure in what you do. If you're lucky, work is fun. For some leaders, solving problems or working as a team is a great time. They do it because it's pure enjoyment. When I ask my clients about finding enjoyment in their work, however, many respond as though this is something out of their control. That is leadersh*t. You may be locked into a prison of routine that has made your work less enjoyable, but that's where metacognition—the ability to step back and watch yourself thinking—is invaluable.

We often fail to appreciate the impact that the workplace has on us. It may be the single most influential force behind quality of life. What did you used to love about your work? Why did you start doing what you do? What gives you the greatest pleasure and how can you do more of it? If your priority as the leader is to make work more enjoyable and to encourage escape and fun within the professional environment, then morale will improve, employees will begin finding their own ways to add pleasure to their work, and everyone will enjoy coming to the office more. It's a virtuous cycle.

I'm not suggesting that every hour at the office will be a party, or that you and your people will be (or should be) playing beer pong in the break room and going on trips to Vegas together. Work will always have some elements of stress and difficulty. Try starting with sustainable changes for yourself, whether that means creative, fun brainstorming sessions; dialing up the "meaning component" of your work; or creating new rules of engagement that breathe new oxygen into the environment for you and everyone else. You will fuel sustainable changes in your organization.

Your Gross Personal Happiness Index

Sometimes, my job as a coach is about reminding leaders to be kinder to themselves, take care of themselves, and not treat themselves as machines. I ask things like, "Are you playing enough?" and "Are you having enough fun?" Organizational culture is not comfortable with those questions, but they are the ones we should be asking. Enjoyment, passion, and purpose go to the heart of what it means to lead effectively. When your bucket is full of energy and passion, it's easy to help others fill their buckets. But when your bucket is nearly empty, it's impossible to marshal the energy and bravery to go first.

Real surprises come when I catch leaders off guard, when they're not worried about the image that they maintain for others. In those less guarded moments, many admit that their work is less fun and joyful than it was when they started, and that they're bored or frustrated. There's no correlation between an executive making more money and him finding more enjoyment in his job. In fact, it's often inversely proportional: higher position equals higher income equals more responsibility, and pressure equals more stress and less pleasure.

I'm not surprised by any of this. Our society is *spiritually* exhausted. This life is hard. We've forgotten about enjoyment as a metric of success. It's about money and growth, but what do those serve? When I started working with Valorie Kondos Field at UCLA, she said, "I haven't won a national title in five years, and I want to see if my leadership is causing that. I'm not having fun anymore." That's the kind of ennui that ends careers and can steer a company right into the ground.

Work should be, above all, a source of passion and fun. When we were children, we would play for endless hours without fatigue, and without stopping until our mothers called us in. We have forgotten that fun—and I mean the giddy, dizzying, grin-so-wide-your-face-aches kind of fun that so many adults are embarrassed to admit to—is a great source of energy. You don't have to teach children to be present. They do it automatically.

They also get it in the Himalayan kingdom of Bhutan. There, the government measures progress by the Gross National Happiness index, which measures not only economic health but also its citizens' peace, security, and contentment. It's brilliant. Each of us would benefit from his or her own Gross Personal Happiness Index—something that regularly monitors our level of joy, fulfillment, passion, and purpose in our work. No one is going to create yours for you; there's no app for that. It's up to you to create your own GPH Index.

One way or another, the workplace is evolving in such a way that personal happiness and replenishment can no longer be ignored. Cathy Benko, a longtime client, friend and bestselling author who calls herself a "sassy redheaded Jersey girl," has seen workplace culture shift completely from her perspective as chief talent officer at Deloitte. "Since the boomers started retiring, you can see the contrast and change in the attitude of the workforce," she says. "The whole flow of information and how one participates in an organization—and, therefore, how you lead—had fundamentally changed. The top-down communications model—word comes down from the boss to his direct reports, then to *their* direct reports, filtering down rung by rung—that's dying.

"Communication, and therefore the culture, is much more transparent and democratic," she continues. "Information can start from any node. Leadership is evolving, in part, in response to the new ways that information flows. The old leadership models were based on control, but now, the leader doesn't have total control. He might have power of the pen—signing someone's compensation—but the workplace has become much more like everyday life. Everyday life is about influencing and persuading. The game has changed and continues to change."

With greater access to information and the breakdown of traditional hierarchies comes a greater call for leaders to listen to their people and to be attentive to their needs. And what they need—what *you* need—above all is the chance to remake work into something restorative, not draining. In the best organizations, the stream both taps and replenishes itself.

LEADERSH*T

Being self-conscious about your and your people's need
for enjoyment and pleasure at work and
insisting that "you're here to work"
means feeling like a slave.

LEADING

Renewing morale, purpose, and productivity
by embracing the idea
that joy is one of the best metrics of a successful company;
finding ways to weave pleasure
into your professional experience.

Essence Is Everything

I've hinted at the concept of essence for some time, but now it's time to get to the heart of the matter. When you combine all the vital states of mind we've discussed—mindful presence, passion, joy, full engagement, authenticity—you get *essence*. Everything in breakthrough leading comes down to a single question:

Are you leading from essence or from ego?

Your essence is who you are when you are at your best. It's that simple. When you are connected to your source, mindfully present, with a clear stream, free of distracting noise, aware of who and what you're serving, authentic and accountable, you are at your best. How does that ideal leader manifest? Are you a hands-on coach helping each team member bring out his or her gifts?

Are you a fearless risk taker stoking the crazy creativity of your followers? That is your essence.

Leading from your essence is leading from what motivates you, what you care about, and the principles and values that you stand for. It's 100 percent pure *you*—undiluted, unfettered, playing fully and without any concerns beyond doing the things that elevate your people to bring forth their best selves. Essence evokes essence. Such total authenticity is instantly clear to the people you're leading, which is why they respond. Honestly, vulnerability, and recognition of others' unique gifts constitute an extremely potent position from which to lead.

Leading from ego has the opposite effect. To lead from ego means that you are trying to meet the expectations of others, seek their approval, protect turf, conceal your own self-doubts, or diminish a rival. Leading becomes a tool to polish your own resume. It's all about you—your position, salary, and credit. It's also a dead end. The culture springs from you. If you are leading from a ravenous ego, your followers will also think only about themselves. Team-work collapses and vision gives way to greed and fear of failure. What kind of results will that produce for your organization?

I'll give you a wonderful example of leading from essence and how it can cascade. I heard this story at the awards banquet celebrating UCLA's 2010 NCAA Women's Gymnastics Championship. After the great John Wooden heard that the team had won the title, he told his dear friend Valorie Kondos Field that he was most proud of how they had won by focusing on doing their work, not on the other team. When the final athlete came off the floor after flawlessly landing her routine in the floor exercise, UCLA's final event at the championship, the team erupted in cheers and tears. When

Miss Val asked the team if that was the moment they knew they had won the championship, they all said, "No, we had no idea. At that moment, we didn't care. We had set a goal to compete against ourselves and land 24 routines out of 24." When the last Bruin landed her routine, they had done what they set out to accomplish.

They had controlled what they could control. Winning the championship was a fortunate consequence of that focus.

To that, Coach Wooden is reported to have said, "That's what I meant by competitive greatness. You achieved competitive greatness."

That is essence at work, flowing from the leader to the led and back.

LEADERSH*T

Leading to serve your own ego, roles,
self-focus, and expectations.

LEADING

Leading from essence, empowering yourself to
be your best and your followers to do the same.

It's Always about Why

This stuff—essence, joy, purpose, replenishing the source of your stream—may appear simple. But I've spent 30 years researching, analyzing, and working with thousands of leaders to make it look that way. Underneath all this lies a deep layer of complexity—human psychology, organizational dynamics, spiritual development, and much more. It can be simple to understand, but its impact is unfathomably complicated. Any organization is an ecosystem in which thousands of moving parts are each influenced by all the others. Because of this, your impact as a leader spreads wider than you may have realized. Eventually, a trickling spring up in northern Minnesota becomes the Mississippi River.

What I ask you to remember is that at the end of the day, when you're filled with questions and doubts about what your role is and how you can fulfill your duties to others while remaining true to yourself, the question that matters most is "Why?" Why do you do what you do? Why does it matter? Why must you lead in a certain way? Why do others follow you?

Dick Eaton says, "I find the asking of 'Why' to be very present in certain companies. It's part of the culture where the leader makes it part of the culture. We should always ask why we're doing something. Introspection is not rewarded in the typical business environment. It's not encouraged. The emphasis is on performance measurements. But reflection is something we need to do more of. We need to teach our leaders to do it and show it."

If you find it difficult to break inertia and act on the advice in this book, begin by asking "Why?" Keep it simple. You say you have challenges? We all have challenges. Someone has an addicted son. Another has a parent with Alzheimer's. You have a direct report who comes to you and says, "My husband left me." Start simply in your drive to clear your stream. Do what you must to recapture the enjoyment in what you do, even if you start in a small way. Journey of a thousand miles, single step . . . you know the drill.

You have always known this. It's ancient, inherited wisdom. Maybe you've just forgotten it or tuned it out—or it got lost in Outlook. Your deep wisdom is like a muscle that atrophies from disuse. You've had it forced deep inside you by the pressures of business. We're not asked to be wise these days. We're asked to be informed, foresighted, tough, and self-sacrificing. But in today's complex, fast-paced, and life-draining word, is there anything more important than wisdom?

What gets in the way of your clarity, presence, and courage? Do you need to rediscover your inner seven-year-old with a pirate hat, a bike, and a thirst for adventure? He's still there, you know. Those parts of us never die; they just go dormant, waiting to be awakened. Have fun, slow down, breathe deeply, tell the truth. Live in pursuit of a goal, build your weak muscles, serve a purpose bigger than yourself. I actually say these things to big-time executives in conference rooms that cost more to decorate than my house cost to buy. When I do it in a way that they can hear, it's remarkable. They remember themselves for the first time in a long time.

Seven Keys

In the end, *Leadersh*t: Rethinking the True Journey to Great Leading* is all about giving you the seven keys to unlocking your essence, the seven Access Points:

- The Stream
- The Empty House
- The Old Bull
- The Source
- The Skipping Stone
- The Storm
- The Trail

These seven concepts for powerfully leading yourself and others are simple enough to be within the reach of everyone reading this book, from Little League coach to parent to C-suite executive. When you clear your stream, get out of your own way, and stop being driven by fear, epistemic closure, noise, ego, or expectations, you don't become a different person, but rather, a better you. You're unencumbered, unhindered, present, sourced, and empowered by meaning. It's your best self—your essence.

Leadersh*t culture tells you that you're broken. It insists you're not leading unless you're running yourself and your people until the tires are bald and the engine throws a rod. That's a lie. None of us is broken. We have everything we need.

I'll give the great Marianne Williamson the last word, because her words are more beautiful than mine. She writes, "Who am I to be brilliant, gorgeous, talented, fabulous? Actually, who are you *not* to be? You are a child of God."

You already have everything you need. Now go use it.

LEADERSH*T

Accepting the idea that you are broken and
that your only value lies in the empty, soulless leading
that today's corporate culture dictates.

LEADING

Finding the adventurous, daring child within you
and bringing that same joy, presence,
and energy to everything you do and everyone you lead.

ACCESS POINTS

The Tale of the Spring

*Questions I've asked myself and others in our lifelong efforts to
discover and lead from essence:*

What are the values (e.g., spirituality, knowledge, integrity, adventure, security, love) that are most important to me?

_____

_____

_____

_____

_____

What would my significant other say are my values (based on my actual behavior)?

_____

_____

_____

_____

_____

Which of my values do I act on each day?

_____

_____

_____

_____

What are the things I love most in my life?

_____

_____

_____

_____

_____

What are my core talents, for which people consistently count on me?

_____

_____

_____

_____

_____

What holds me back from truly being myself at work? As a leader?

_____

_____

_____

_____

_____

What would it make possible if those I lead really understood more about my passions, talents, fears, concerns, etc.?

_____

_____

_____

_____

_____

What can I do, every day, to encourage the full and honest self-expression in those I lead?

_____

_____

_____

_____

_____

ACKNOWLEDGMENTS

From my earliest memories, I've loved the written word. It's been a lifelong dream to consider myself a contributor to this alluring arena. To make this dream a reality, I owe thanks to many.

Thanks and love to my family for their love, sacrifice, and encouragement, all of which have allowed me to pursue this passion with zeal.

Next, thanks to the incredible team at The Foster Mobley Group (FMG), talented professionals committed to assisting leaders and companies build and enact healthy, sustainable transformation. This has been my work home for the past 27 years and has, in many ways, defined a large part of my professional life. These dedicated colleagues provided ideas, lift, feedback, and "air cover" to write both this book and my doctoral dissertation in the span of three years. I am grateful for the sacrifices you made to allow me to pursue both important dreams.

Finally, I thank my teachers, mentors, clients, and friends, who have allowed me to learn alongside them. Many are mentioned in specific stories in this book: Maritza Montiel and Cathy Benko of Deloitte, Paul Viviano of Alliance HealthCare Services, my sister Dede Henley, Andrew Hayek of Surgical Care Affiliates, Joe Mello of DaVita and Valorie Kondos Field and Kelly Inouye-Perez of UCLA. Many more are unnamed here yet no less important to me. To these teachers, including the thousands of leaders and hundreds of companies with whom I've worked over the past three decades to hone my craft and sharpen my beliefs, I am incredibly grateful.

ABOUT THE AUTHOR

Dr. Foster Mobley is the founder and Chief Executive Officer of The Foster Mobley Group (www.fmgleading.com), a leadership and change consultancy in Newport Beach, California. He has been a thought leader and leading practitioner in the development of healthy leaders, teams and companies for over three decades. His client list includes some of the world's most admired companies, including Citicorp, Deloitte, Disney, Nokia and numerous leading health care companies. Foster's passion for, and work in developing high performance individual and team performance in elite-level athletics earned him two NCAA Championship rings in 2010. Foster holds a Bachelor of Arts degree from UCLA, and MBA and doctoral degrees from Pepperdine University. He is Chairman of Kids Global Outreach (www.kidsglobaloutreach.org), a non-profit organization committed to supporting sustainable improvements in the lives of children across the globe. Foster resides in Southern California with his wife Cathy, and has three grown children.